METAPHYSICAL PRIMER

A Guide To Understanding Metaphysics

BY
JANE L. ROBERTSON and
DEBORAH L. HUGHES

METAGNOSIS®

METAPHYSICAL PRIMER,
A Guide To Understanding Metaphysics

by Jane L. Robertson, D.D.
    Deborah L. Hughes

Metagnosis[R]
P.O. Box 11123, Boulder, CO 80301-0002
Copyright 1991 by Jane L. Robertson and Deborah L. Hughes

Library of Congress Cataloging-in-Publication Data

Robertson, Jane, 1946
Hughes, Deborah, 1950

Rev. Ed. Metaphysical Primer, A Guide To
Understanding Metaphysics, 1995
Metaphysical Primer, A Guide To
Understanding Metaphysics, 1991
Rev. ed. of: A Layman's Guide To Understanding Metaphysics,
1990
Includes index.
ISBN 1-879203-02-2

Printed and bound in the United States

ACKNOWLEDGEMENT

A warm acknowledgement goes out to all the students who have attended Metagnosis^R workshops and classes, used the meditation tapes, and enthusiastically read the books. Thank you for your input and suggestions, but most of all for your warmth and friendship. In addition, thank you also for your letters of praise of the first edition of this text. We hope that you will recommend this revised and updated version to others who share your interest in learning and growing through the metaphysical teachings.

We dedicate this book to all of you who are truly seeking to become the empowered, spiritual beings we are all meant to be.

CONTENTS

About The Authors   **i**

Introduction   **iii**

Chapter 1:   **WHY STUDY METAPHYSICS?**   **1**
Definition of Metaphysics; Purpose of Metaphysical
Study; Eastern & Western Systems; Metaphysics is
Not a Religion; Personal Relationships; Using
Metaphysics; Conclusion

Chapter 2:   **THE BASIC METAPHYSICAL**   **9**
                   PRINCIPLES
How To Begin Your Quest; You Are The Director Of
Your Life;   Mind As The Builder/Destroyer; Life
Experience As Lessons; The Principle of Universal Law;
The Psychic Mind As A Tool;   Past Life Therapy;
Consciousness; Conclusion

Chapter 3:   **BASIC UNIVERSAL LAWS**   **27**
Universal Law, What Is It?; Law of One; Law of Mind;
Law of Love; Law of Duality; Law of Karma; Law of
Reincarnation; Law of Attraction; Law of Return;
Conclusion; Suggested Exercises

Chapter 4:   RELIGION AND METAPHYSICS 45
Where Is God In Metaphysics?; Your Personal Belief
System; Definition of Religion; "Satan" As A
Personification of Negativity; Heaven and Hell; The
Psychic Mind As A Spiritual Gift; Savior or Master
Teacher?; Conclusion

**Chapter 5:   METAPHYSICAL VIEW OF   58
                DEATH AND IMMORTALITY**
Your Many Bodies; What Happens At Death?; Near Death
Experiences; Reincarnation of the Soul; Evolution of
the Soul; Perspective on Understanding Death; Conclusion

Chapter 6:   DREAMS IN METAPHYSICS   69

**Chapter 7:   TECHNIQUES USED IN THE   84
                STUDY OF METAPHYSICS**
Value of Concentration, Visualization and Meditation;
Using The Techniques; A Concentration Exercise;
Visualization; Meditation; Purpose of Metaphysical
Exercises; Conclusion

**Chapter 8:   THE PSYCHIC EXPERIENCE   93
                THROUGH   READINGS   AND
                TEACHERS**

What Is Truth?; Psychic Fairs; Readings And What To
Look For In A Reader; Types of Readings; A Tip About
Readings; Metaphysical Teachers; The New Age Label;
Conclusion

Chapter 9:   **APPLYING PRACTICAL**   **112**
                 METAPHYSICS IN DAILY LIFE
Metaphysical Study Affects You On A Physical Level;
Centers of Energy Within You; Chart: Process of Higher
Energies Flowing Through The Centers; How To Apply
Metaphysical Ideas In Everyday Life; Conclusion

Chapter 10:   **GLOSSARY**   **122**
This Glossary translates "metaphysical jargon"
into plain English for your better understanding
of metaphysical texts.

**A COMBINED BIBLIOGRAPHY and READING
LIST**   **134**

TABLE OF CHARTS

Tracking Effects of the Universal Laws   **43**
How To Set Up Your Dream Journal   **77-78**
Higher Energies Flowing Through The Centers   **115**

ABOUT THE AUTHORS

JANE L. ROBERTSON, D.D.

Jane's background incudes a doctorate in comparative religions and esoteric philosophy from a metaphysical church seminary in Pennsylvania. She was ordained in 1983 and decided to pursue her ministry in teaching self-help and metaphysical workshops as well as giving spiritual counseling.

Since 1978 Jane has taught classes in metaphysics and given lectures and workshops throughout the U.S. Concise and easy to understand metaphysical texts were not available when she began teaching, so she wrote her own. Due to the large amount of writing compiled over the years of teaching, she established a small publishing company, Metagnosis[R] Publications, Inc. (now Metagnosis [R]) which was formed in 1990.

Jane formerly worked as a magazine journalist and in public relations. She has also taught philosophy at the community college level. Presently she is publisher/editor of MetaGnosis[R].

DEBORAH L. HUGHES

Deborah has written magazine articles, but prefers to pursue her love of writing novels. In 1985 she authored a United Nations Proclamation For The Year of the Child at the request of Richard Salmon of the International Environmental Education Foundation. This proclamation was presented to the U.N. Secretary General that same year.

Deborah began her spiritual quest in 1987 and is a student of "A Course In Miracles." She has also studied a broad range of general metaphysical studies with Jane.

Since she saw the difficulty in wading through "metaphysical jargon" when she began her studies, she was able to sense the need for a clear and practical foundation of metaphysical teaching material. She is the author with the original idea for this book to be an aid to people new to metaphysical thought, and a great reference for those who have studied metaphysics for awhile.

Through her keen eye for editing and focused ideas she has helped to keep the text at the beginning level for new students, or for people interested in knowing what metaphysics is all about.

ABOUT METAGNOSIS[R]

MetaGnosis[R] is a publishing company dedicated to producing metaphysical, self-help, spiritual books, meditation tapes, and workshops that provide insight and guidance for your spiritual and personal growth. It was formed in 1990 as Metagnosis Publications from the vision of Jane L. Robertson, D.D. who felt that metaphysical information need not be complex and difficult to read or comprehend. From her studies of philosophy in college, and in the metaphysical church seminary, she realized that a variety of esoteric systems from many cultures are available to access the ancient wisdom teachings. Utilizing her ability to create a synthesis of diverse sources of information, she began writing lessons and workshops, of metaphysical/spiritual knowledge. Thus, MetaGnosis was created as a vehicle for sharing this knowledge with those who are seeking to understand the deeper meaning of life.

In addition to metaphysical books, MetaGnosis[R] offers workshops and classes, presented by Dr. Robertson, throughout the United States. Meditation tapes are currently in production. It is our great hope that you enjoy learning about metaphysical subjects through this vehicle of knowledge called MetaGnosis[R].

INTRODUCTION

The pressures of modern times are enormous. Many of us suffer the effects of urban crowding and watch with dismay as traditional family values fall to a high divorce rate and the devastation of drugs. On a world scale we see widespread famine, disease and the ravages of war. Yet there is a stirring of change with the new attitudes of the Soviet Union, the destruction of the Berlin Wall, and the great progress being made in holistic health. In these times of change we long to make our lives better and to understand the deeper meaning of life.

Some seek comfort and understanding through an exploration of psychology, science, philosophy or religion, while others turn to the study of metaphysics. Everyday there is a dazzling array of new books on the market about metaphysical ideas such as holistic healing, crystals, past lives, and the power of the mind to heal or direct energy.

Yet for the person discovering these subjects, the terminology and the basic ideas presented are foreign, and it is easy to become discouraged while wading through metaphysical jargon. The interest in the subject may be great, but the basic concepts must be understood before any of the ideas can be put into practical use. We wrote this book to help the beginning student and general public understand metaphysical principles in layman's language.

Metaphysics is defined as "mind beyond physical reality." It is a vast subject encompassing psychology, philosophy, theology, physics and science, but takes these subjects one step further into deeper levels of understanding. In learning the basic metaphysical laws, which are mental but work within the natural laws of Earth, you take greater control of your life. You learn that the effects of your thoughts, words and actions have a negative or positive influence in your life.

The purpose of this book is to present these basic metaphysical laws and offer safe, practical methods for their use. By working with metaphysical principles in daily living through the knowledge of the effects of your thoughts, you realize that you are not a "victim" of circumstances. Rather, you will find that life follows a natural pattern according to the conscious and subconscious thoughts of the individual. Becoming consciously aware of that thinking is a basic principle of metaphysics.

Introduction

The text explains how to handle questions that arise from friends and family when you begin to study metaphysics, as well as how to work with the similarities and differences between metaphysics and religion. The study of metaphysics should not be viewed as a threat to your present belief system, but rather as a means to expanding that belief system and enriching it. There is no need for the student to change religion, friends or spouse to explore the realm of metaphysical ideas, though this is a common misperception often made by people exploring metaphysics.

Like any other study undertaken, metaphysics does not create problems, but it may bring personal problems to the surface that have been suppressed for sometime. The study of psychology, philosophy or theology would do the same thing.

It is our goal to guide you, the new student or seeker, through the maze of metaphysical information and give you a solid foundation of investigation, study, and practical use of metaphysics in daily living. We speak to you from the experiences of the teacher, and the curiosity of the student. We are all seekers of Truth. We wish to present a new tool, the study of metaphysics, that will shed light on the changes and turmoil of our modern world.

The Authors:
Jane L. Robertson, D.D.
Deborah L. Hughes

CHAPTER 1

WHY STUDY METAPHYSICS?

DEFINITION OF METAPHYSICS

Language imposes limits on concepts. The precise definition of metaphysics does not begin to explain the vastness of the subject. It is a concept that has no limits, no prescribed boundaries.

With that in mind, let us define metaphysics according to the limiting language of today. The word physics means the study of matter and energy, while meta means to transcend or "see the situation behind something." Metaphysics, then, is the study of matter and energy beyond the physical plane to other dimensions. Many of you may be familiar with metaphysics through studying philosophy in college, which discussed the metaphysics of the philosophers, meaning how they viewed the cosmology of the universe, or how things "came to be."

The metaphysics given in this book expands that philosophical view to include space-time relationships, such as the theory of reincarnation and communication with interdimensional beings called "channeling," The study of metaphysics assumes that the power of mental energy is immense, and that every individual has the ability to use his or her mental energies to live life to the fullest.

The power of the mind has been demonstrated over the years in experiments with: telepathy, one mind communicating with another through thought; telekinesis, mental energy moving objects; and clairvoyance, the ability to "see" the past or future events of an individual's life. Many people come to the study of metaphysics not so much because of an interest in mental powers, but in search of a deeper meaning of life.

While VCR's, computer games, and climbing the corporate ladder of success hold the interest of many people, you may come to a time in life when these things seem superficial and empty. Metaphysics, with its concepts of the ability of the mind to bring energies from inner dimensions down to the physical, life beyond death through reincarnation, and the healing power of the mind, offers answers to difficult questions about the meaning of life. Some of these questions are: "what is my purpose for being here?; do we really have only one life to perfect ourselves?; if there is a just God, then why is there so much suffering in the world?; and are there truly Higher Beings with whom we can communicate for guidance?"

Perhaps a study of psychology, theology or philosophy helps answer a few of these questions, but there is always a nagging feeling that something is missing. That something is a recognition of other dimensions beyond the physical plane that are orderly and affect daily life. When the belief system in which you were raised no longer adequately answers all of your questions about life, you are ready to experience personal growth on a new level. Often it is at this time in life that an interest is developed in metaphysical ideas.

PURPOSE OF METAPHYSICAL STUDY

The purpose of studying metaphysics is to develop personal growth through the process of daily living. Success in relationships, career fulfillment, and optional health is possible when you change your belief system to an expanded awareness beyond the narrow day-to-day existence most of us live. Spiritual growth is also possible through development of a calmer nature, open and honest communication, and unconditional love for humanity, Earth and all things.

In essence, the purpose of metaphysical study is to help you overcome limited thinking and become all you can be. The method used to do this is a study of ancient theories of how the universe was formed, how it operates and man's purpose in it. Exercises in concentration, visualization and meditation are part of the studies to help you focus and become comfortable in working with your mind.

EASTERN AND WESTERN SYSTEMS

Many people believe that metaphysics is the study of only Eastern philosophies, however this is incorrect. While the East offers a wealth of information on reincarnation, meditation and health, the Western civilization is rich in its own metaphysics. Kabbalistic studies, an ancient system that developed out of the Jewish culture; Gnosticism, an eclectic system with strong hermetic teachings; the Earth Religions such as Native American, Wicca; and the Grail Mysteries, are excellent metaphysical sources geared to Western thinking.

Ideally, the study of metaphysics will include some teachings of each. Truth is found in all philosophies and cultures, and no one person, book or belief system holds every one of the Ancient Truth Teachings. Because metaphysics covers all philosophies and beliefs of ancient cultures, it draws upon a vast system of knowledge and wisdom. It is a spiritual elixir for humanity, as it recognizes that spiritual (not religious) and personal growth go hand in hand.

A metaphysician lives life from an expanded view of the world, due to his belief that the only limitations are those he places upon himself. Life becomes a giant laboratory where he, as the scientist, works the experiments of daily living. Like any scientist, he will have his share of failed experiments which in today's world translate into divorce, broken friendships, loss of a job or career. However, an experiment that failed does not invalidate the scientist.

What is gained from a failed experiment is valuable knowledge and new insights about relationships, work and self-esteem. With this new understanding, the life scientist can go on to succeed in future experiments such as a remarriage, new friendships, or a career more suited to his goals.

METAPHYSICS IS NOT A RELIGION

Since metaphysics encompasses such a broad scope, it will include some study of the philosophies and theology of world religions. For this reason, it is often accused of being a religion, which it is not. However, the exploration of metaphysical ideas threatens anyone who insists on living life by the dogma and doctrine of a particular religion.

People who live by a certain religious practice may not realize that religion can be anything from art to psychology, if the individual holds on to it with enough conviction and faith. Based on this definition, metaphysics can become your religion if you refuse to accept other belief systems as valid, whether they be religious, scientific or psychological.

Because of this general misunderstanding of what metaphysics is, you may encounter criticism from friends, your spouse, or well-meaning relatives who do not like such an expansive view of life. You will also have to battle with yourself to keep from becoming dogmatic about your new interest in metaphysical ideas. It is easy enough when asked what metaphysics is to say, "the study of the power of mind beyond the physical world." They will probably probe you to tell them more, which you may be eager to do. Remember, however, that everyone is at a different level of personal and spiritual growth. They may not be ready to hear about theories of reincarnation, mental healing, or mediumship.

Respect their belief systems, whatever that may be, and expect respect for your own, even if it is in its formative stages. It is part of human nature to want to share new ideas with friends and family, but if these ideas are far removed from their view of the world, it is better to keep quiet until you have a good grasp on the subject. By then you will have become comfortable with your new way of looking at life, and will not feel the need to convert everyone to your way of thinking.

Keep in mind that it is also part of human nature to want to make everyone believe as you do. The reasoning is that if everyone believes as you do, then you are right and those who do not believe as you must be wrong. It then becomes your duty to convert anyone who does not see things your way so that you do not have to face the possibility of being wrong.

This is the mindset of many people, including new metaphysical students, and you are certain to encounter some of this kind of thinking. Restrain your enthusiasm for converting the world and work on yourself so that you no longer have a "them and us" attitude.

PERSONAL RELATIONSHIPS

A conflict of ideas can cause strain in relationships. There are people whose spouses became convinced that metaphysics was responsible for destroying their marriages. Problems in the marriage were developing long before their spouses began reading metaphysical material. The study of metaphysics stimulates individual thinking and promotes questions about religion and personal relationships. As you become more of an individual, you begin to reject old habits and find new ways of viewing the world and personal relationships.

Unfortunately this self-growth can cause repressed problems to surface. These may threaten a spouse, friends or family members who have been content to ignore these friction points. The same thing could happen, however, if you studied any other self-growth subject. Metaphysics should not be used as a scapegoat for personal problems.

USING METAPHYSICS

There is a tendency among those recently acquainted with metaphysical material to intellectualize rather than to practice the principles. This creates a self-righteous attitude that is an excuse not to face life. If you adopt this practice, metaphysical study will become no more than a new doctrine for you. You will not be living life to the fullest, which is what the study is supposed to teach you.

Often new students use phrases like, "It's my karma to have a bad temper. I was so mistreated in a past life that I inherited an ill nature this life." That is absolute nonsense! The individual using this excuse has not learned two of the basic principles of metaphysics--free will and personal responsibility. While past lives, and even the past in this life affect you, there is always the opportunity to make things right. You have free will to correct things by a change in attitude and by performing acts of restitution.

There is no doubt that the serious study of metaphysics will change your disposition and outlook on life. Self-growth always causes you to look at the value and sincerity of personal relationships, which may produce a "weeding of the garden of relationships." What is left, however, will be real friends who respect your right to explore new ideas.

CONCLUSION

Any new way of looking at things is considered dangerous by people who do not want to expand their consciousness. Democracy is still considered a dangerous idea in some parts of the world. You will have to decide for yourself whether or not the study of metaphysics is right for you. If you decide to pursue it, you will be given the keys to control your own life, create your own world, and the opportunity to become the successful and happy individual you want to be.

CHAPTER 2

BASIC METAPHYSICAL PRINCIPLES

HOW TO BEGIN YOUR QUEST

When you are attracted to metaphysical subjects, you may not know where to begin with your search for information. While bookstores are helpful, they cannot direct you to one book that will offer a basic outline of metaphysical ideas. What they do offer is a good supply of three types of metaphysical material: (1) books written from personal experiences; (2) books of channeled material from inter-dimensional beings; and (3) books of various philosophies that teach strictly from their viewpoint. Each of the books in this latter group often has its own terminology and includes such ideas as theosophy, the Eastern systems of metaphysical study, and courses of study from metaphysical organizations.

Within these three groups you will find many subjects to investigate, such as healing, herbs, crystals, telepathy, psychometry, meditation, and channeling to list only a few. These books and subjects all have a common thread running through them, however, and that is the basic metaphysical principles. In the following chapter, we will present a clear explanation of these principles which are the basis of all metaphysical teachings.

YOU ARE THE DIRECTOR OF YOUR LIFE

No outside force directs your actions and you are NOT a victim of anything! This basic metaphysical principle underlies all that is written on metaphysics. What is implied in the above statement is that nothing external controls you. There is a part, an internal essence of you, that IS directing your thinking and your perception of the world.

So who is this controller and who put it in charge? The answer is the "Higher Self" within you, who has all knowledge and knows what your path in life is. This concept brings up some interesting questions and conflicts, for it is the principle of a "Higher Self" that often labels metaphysics as being a religion. Unfortunately this concept is misinterpreted as saying that metaphysics negates a Divine Being or higher source of wisdom. The difference is the metaphysical perception of that source of wisdom.

Metaphysics teaches that there is one Deity, whatever your religious belief perceives that Being to be, and that

Being is within you rather than apart from you. The part of you that is ever in contact with that Deity is the Higher Self. The Higher Self is constantly receiving energies from the Deity. These energies not only sustain your physical body, but also direct you to the life experiences you need for spiritual and personal growth.

If you are always receiving such wonderful directions, then why doesn't life flow smoothly without suffering and mistakes? The answer is that you have a marvelous gift from the Deity called "free will." You are free to choose whatever actions you desire, negative or positive, and nothing interferes with that choice.

Obviously you are not always hearing direct messages from the Higher Self. They come to you through a valuable receiving unit that also acts as an obstacle to these communications: your lower self. Your lower self is your personality, that part of you whom you identify as yourself and whom you know the best: your desires, passions, fears and doubts. Your personality uses free will to the maximum and ignores your Higher Self messages, because it is unconscious of your Higher Self until you consciously begin to pursue your spiritual path. Unfortunately your personality self may choose an entirely different path, one that is not always free of pain and suffering.

For example, you decide you are gaining too much weight. You cannot get into all of your clothes, and that makes you disgusted with your overeating. You decide to go on a diet. That decision is an indication that you have received a message from your Higher Self telling you it is time to put some self-discipline into your life, and a diet will be a way to do this.

However, there is a party tonight at a friend's house nd you feel obligated to go. You promise yourself that you will eat lightly and not eat sweets. The lower self has not rebelled at that promise yet, because it is waiting until you get to your friend's house and see delicious pastries she has set out, plus chocolates, your favorite. The Higher Self message is still being received, though, and you carefully maneuver yourself to the raw vegetable plate instead of the chocolate tray. The lower self is getting restless, because it looked forward all week to this party and now some silly part of you is interfering with its desires.

Finally, the craving is too much and you say to yourself, "one or two won't hurt," while you delicately pluck a couple of mint cremes off the tray. The lower self likes this power and control it has over you. In fact, it likes it so much, it decides you should have some pastries to accompany the chocolate. You avoid the urge for the pastries for ten minutes by engaging in conversation to take your mind off the goodies. But the more you try to forget them, the pushier the desires of the lower self get, until finally you consent to have one more.

This one is more delicious than all the others together, so at last you give in and tell yourself you will start the diet tomorrow. After all, these things take time and you do not want to rush into anything. The lower self, through your strong desire system, has just overridden the messages from the Higher Self.

You are still the director of your life, however, and no outside force made you eat the chocolate or pastries. Your friend did not put those on the table to sabotage your diet. The conflict of messages within yourself caused the overeating. The personality's old habit of overindulging in food negated the Higher Self message of self-discipline, which was communicated in the form of intuition or conscience.

The example is a double conflict, for the new student will say, "I would also suffer if I listened to my Higher Self and dieted, because dieting is frustrating and craving for a favorite food hurts!" Yes, that is true, but overall the diet would take off the excess weight, improve your health, and the cravings would be brought under control. More importantly, the exercise of self-discipline required to diet would strengthen you to use self-discipline needed in other areas of your life.

The first metaphysical principle can be summed up in the words *personal responsibility.* "You are the director of your life" means you make the decisions, right or wrong. You act on those decisions, and you suffer or are made better by your decisions.

No outside circumstance or situation forces you to make a decision against your free will, because you always have a choice. You may choose **not** to make any decision and let things go as they will, or you may make a different decision. It does not matter which you ultimately react to, the Higher Self or lower self. YOU are always the decision maker, and therefore always in control of your life.

It is both comforting and scary to be the one totally responsible for you. While it is a relief to know that you are not a puppet being forced to do either painful or pleasurable things, it is also frightening to realize you can no longer blame someone else. Some faceless God, a parent, a spouse, or society is not responsible for all the bad things that have happened to you. For whatever reason, you chose to do the things you did, and you control your life.

THE PRINCIPLE OF UNIVERSAL LAW

An essential foundation of metaphysics is the principle of Universal Law. This set of laws rule the Universe just as natural laws rule the Earth. On Earth water freezes and becomes ice, or fire changes the physical structure of matter.

Universal Laws allow the Universe to balance and function as a unit. These laws are exacting, perfect, and rule your life as surely as your heartbeat keeps you alive. They are the essence of the Universe, and they cannot be negated.

No one Universal law is more or less important than another. There is never a time when a Universal Law is not working. For example, the Law of Mind states that a universal intelligence exists which is substance without form. This substance is the Universal Subconscious Mind, and it is shared by all humanity all the time. It is the same substance that your mind uses to create thought forms. Because this formless substance of the Law of Mind exists, you are able to create your own life situations and manifest your desires or fears through the process of thinking. There are many Universal Laws. Chapter 3 will discuss more of them in depth.

MIND AS THE BUILDER/DESTROYER

The idea of you as the established director of your life leads to another basic metaphysical principle: your mind as the builder or destroyer of your life circumstances.

The cornerstone of metaphysics is that mind is one of the most powerful tools available to you. Scientists tell us that the potential of the mind is almost unlimited, and that we use only a small portion of its vast energy. Various experiments in telepathic communication, telekinesis and clairvoyance have been performed in parapsychology labs and universities. Yet, the everyday mind power of the average individual is not truly understood and appreciated.

The language of the mind is symbols and images. According to metaphysical teachings, your thoughts form images or symbols in a substance called "the Universal Subconscious Mind" or C.G. Jung's concept of the "collective unconscious." Thought creates. That is, your thoughts have a life of their own within this inner dimension of universal mind, and they attract other like thoughts, thereby creating a larger thought form. This is in keeping with the metaphysical idea that everything has consciousness, including thought.

Every time you do something, you visualize it in your mind before you perform the action. Things you do automatically are done from a series of mental images you are not aware of, and you perform the action. When something becomes large enough, such as a fetus growing in the womb, it has to come forth into the physical world. A thought, which has become strong enough, also must manifest.

For example, you are sitting at your typewriter thinking about a coffee break. You begin making errors and getting restless thinking about how good a cup of coffee would taste. You finally have to get up and have that cup of coffee. By the action of getting the coffee, you have manifested your thought form or mental image of the coffee.

The power of thought is vast and is not limited to physical desires. It also covers psychological areas of your life such as relationships or job security.

Let's suppose you want a new job. Mental building works off three basic principles: (1) the idea or thought; (2) the desire put towards the idea; (3) release of the idea or thought into the Universal Subconscious Mind. You have the idea of a new job, so you begin to think more and more about this, visualizing yourself in a new job situation. Then you forget about it for awhile because other things in daily life take your interest.

The mind energy spent thinking about a new job was not lost. It created the thought forms to attract the new job to you. You hear about a new position at another company. You go for an interview and are hired.

But be careful what you wish for as it just might come true! You now have your new job. However, it soon proves to be no more fulfilling than your last job. Why is this? Because you did not think specifically about what you wanted the new job to be.

Qualities that are important in this situation are: (1) the type of people you would like to work with, (2) the salary you would accept, and (3) the kind of work you most want to do.

The example of the mind's ability to manifest a new job brings up another concept of the mind as builder. There are always two sides to every idea, the negative and the positive. The mind can also be a destroyer. That is, your misunderstanding of situations and people can destroy you through ill health due to resentment or anger, and psychological imbalance.

If you want a better job situation, but you feel you are not good enough or do not deserve it, you will block your ability to manifest the new job. Your self-doubt and lack of confidence are the barrier to your new position. Such self-made barriers may have nothing to do with your ability to do the work or with your need for better employment. Your attitude about yourself stops the flow of mental energy that will bring you the desired situation.

Worse yet, if you are able to force the attraction of a new job to yourself, you may lose it because you cannot get along with your new co-workers, or the employer, or keep up with the work. Again, this could happen because of your poor self-esteem.

Now, the first basic metaphysical principle comes into play, personal responsibility. There is in all probability nothing wrong with your new co-workers or the type of work, but your own lack of self-worth can create outward conflicts. How you think about yourself and your circumstances crates or destroys.

When you take this concept to a broader level, you can see how the thinking of masses of people, and particularly the leaders of nations has the power to create peace and harmony or to destroy through self-centered attitudes and greed. Through the power of your thinking, you limit or expand your personal life and the world.

After learning about the power of thought and the mind's potential, many students begin to feel guilty about the way they have perceived or thought about things in the past. These feelings are perfectly natural. Just remember that nothing is beyond your reach when you decide to change your attitude. Thought is faster than the speed of light, and once you decide to view yourself, others, and your life from a more positive outlook, things begin to happen in your life to make it better.

Do not let mistakes of the past ruin your present or future. Do something now and plan for the future. Rectify any harm you may have caused others in the past, but if that is not possible, then be aware of the needs of others now and in the future. Those things that you cannot change are done, and you, with your new thinking, are a different person now than you were then. In learning to work with your mind you must learn to forgive, and that begins with forgiving yourself.

One final word on the mind as builder or destroyer. You do not have the right to create a thought that causes harm to another person or binds another person to you. Such thoughts will come back to harm their creator. *You are just as responsible for what you build or destroy with thought as you are with actions.*

LIFE EXPERIENCE AS LESSONS

The metaphysical view of life is that your daily experiences are a series of lessons to help you grow, and this includes both the pleasant and the difficult times of your life.

Imagine Earth as a giant schoolroom and your Higher Self as the Teacher who will instruct you, through your daily life situations. Some of these lessons are unconditional love, caring for the Earth, tolerance, patience, and learning to flow with life rather than trying to force your life to go according to your stubborn will. Of course, there are times when you need to use force to accomplish something, but the lesson is to use force in a positive manner and be able to discern when to use it and when to restrain yourself.

Balance is one of the greatest lessons in life. You are mainly ruled by your emotions, your lower self, and it is the balancing of your emotions that will harmonize your life. Each moment of life offers you opportunities to express the most positive part of yourself. However, there are times when raising your voice, in a controlled manner, (not a temper tantrum) is necessary. For example, if you are disciplining a pet, a strong "No" to an unacceptable action is useful. If you are harassed by a telemarketing sales person, who will not accept "No," you have the right to express in a firm tone that you meant "No," and if he continues to harass you, you will take action against the company. Use of a negative response for a specific purpose when a positive response will not work, is alright, as long as you balance the negative emotions with the positive. That is, do not allow negative responses to become your normal behavior.

New students sometimes mistake the idea of balancing the emotions for suppressing or denying the emotional nature. The metaphysical principle of balance does not mean becoming a robot, strictly intellectual and non-feeling. Balance means to *respond* with your emotions rather than to react.

When you respond to your life experiences, you make the choice to be happy, sad or ambivalent. However, when you react, there is no choice, only a surge of energy that is usually out of control and can do more harm than good.

The purpose of metaphysics is to make you think and respond from a thinking, choice-making aspect of yourself.

While the emotions give us a great deal of pleasure, and that is good, they also give us a great deal of unnecessary pain. A certain amount of pain is needed to learn in life, but so many lives are full of needless pain because the emotional nature is out of control. The emotional nature merely provides lessons from which you can learn and reap great personal growth. It should not be your master.

A serious problem that can arise from the misunderstanding of the principle of life as a series of lessons is false guilt over illness. Many new students mistakenly think of disease as a harsh lesson imposed upon them by the Universe or their Higher Selves to punish them for some fictitious "bad" deed they have committed in the past. While it is true that illness, like any other life experience, is a lesson, it is not true that you attract illness for punishment.

Any illness is a sign that the body needs rest, relaxation, and often more importantly, emotional support. Health encompasses not only drugs, therapies and surgery, which are needed tools in many situations, but also a change in lifestyle, change of diet and a change in your perception of your relationships, job, and personal belief system.

The idea of life lessons is not to justify disease and certainly not to see it as punishment. The proper approach is to understand that all illness is a part of life experience that can be used to evaluate your approach to life, and it can be used as a growing experience.

Your body is simply telling you it is time to change some things, perhaps many things, about your lifestyle.

The time of healing is a time of introspection, to survey your habits and attitudes. It is also a time to help others who are also hurting, physically or emotionally.

HIGHER MIND AND PSYCHIC MIND ENERGIES

Many people become interested in the study of metaphysics because they are attracted by what is called "psychic power." There is a tendency among people new to metaphysical teachings to think that becoming psychic is what metaphysics is all about. Unfortunately this is a misunderstanding. It draws people to metaphysical studies for the wrong reasons. They want to see themselves "above" everyone else since they can read minds, see the future, or tell someone about past lives. These are all tempting talents that lure the student. But any good metaphysical teacher will put the new students ego in perspective when she tells the individual that "all people are psychic."

The so called psychic part of your mind is in you and every other human being. It is part of your innate being, and you use it on a very shallow basis when you respond to your intuition or "gut feelings" about something. The metaphysical sciences teach you to tap into your psychic mind through the disciplines of concentration exercises, visualization techniques, and meditation.

It is only when you learn to attune your mind to a fine point of concentration that you can use your psychic mind at will. Remember, however, that although the psychic mind is a lower level of the mind's potential, it is essential that you learn to control and use your psychic mind power. The more important goal is that you learn to raise your consciousness above the psychic mind to what is known as the "higher mind."

Higher mind energies are more difficult to access at will, but they are more effective in use and are not tainted with the emotions of the lower psychic mind. Higher Mind is accessed through meditation and in deep trance states. It can also be referred to as your Higher Self, or superconscious mind. The messages from Higher Mind are more accurate because the Higher Self is not concerned with the emotional reaction of the situation, but rather the facts and solutions.

CONSCIOUSNESS

A major theme running through all metaphysical texts is the idea that everything has consciousness, including the nature kingdoms of vegetable, animal, and mineral. Consciousness to metaphysicians means self-awareness, however minimal that might appear to humans. Everything has an atomic structure and each atom has a consciousness of its own. Therefore all things must possess consciousness at least at a minimal level.

It is easy to see consciousness in animals as they respond to our voices and affection. You communicate with your pet by talking to it, but at the same time you are thinking about, or visualizing, what you want it to do. While you are speaking and thinking, you are also feeling emotion towards your pet. The pet picks up on all three methods of communication, but it is particularly responsive to thought and feeling, even though it has learned voice command.

It is more difficult to think of plants and rocks having self-awareness. Studies of plants, of course, over the past several years have proven they respond to vibrations of thought and music, so you can see that plants do show awareness. Your plants will respond to the vibration of your voice, but they will mainly respond to your thoughts, negative and positive. They essentially respond to the feeling energy you put forth when you think about them, or care for them.

However, what about a rock? A rock has "mineral consciousness," even though that does not give it the ability to think, speak, or move without assistance. It has individuality just as plants and animals do. Mineral consciousness has come to the forefront with the awareness that quartz crystals are programmable by thought. They can be empowered with specific healing energies, or for the purpose of increasing and refining spiritual energies in the body. There are foundation minerals such as granite or iron that have the consciousness of solid matter to be used for building and holding Earth together.

What all this means to a metaphysician is that, if indeed all things have consciousness and everything shares the same Universal Subconscious Mind, then it is possible to communicate with anything through the process of thought.

Telepathic communication with animals and plants has been proven. You know that your cat or dog will come to you if you think about it long enough. A plant will live or die according to the thoughts of love or dislike projected towards it. Everything emits a vibration, as science has proven, including thought. Through thought you can mentally connect with other vibrations, and therefore communicate with them. Your communication may be receiving the rudimentary feelings of your pets, or the needs of your plants to be watered or fed, but it is still a form of communicating.

To the metaphysical student, the whole world is alive and vibrant with energy, or vibrations. It is a matter of learning to connect your mind with the mind of the animal, plant, or mineral to understand its needs and relationship with humanity.

The ability to connect your mind to another consciousness is similar to learning a different language. You must learn the "words" of that new language and then translate them into your language to be able to comprehend the message. The language of the nature kingdoms is images and feelings. It is also part of your language.

Communicating with the natural kingdoms demonstrates that you are not separate from anything in the world. All things are interconnected through thoughts and feelings. It is important to realize, too, that nothing remains static, and everything is growing in awareness.

Nothing is dead or inanimate to metaphysical thinking, and with this knowledge comes the responsibility of respecting, and caring for the consciousness of all species and Earth. As you become conscious of the needs of plants, animals, and minerals to be loved and encouraged to learn and grow, you will appreciate them for their own level of consciousness. You will become truly at one with Mother Earth giving and receiving her bountiful energies.

IN CONCLUSION

Metaphysics is a vast subject, and the basic principles in this chapter are only a few of the more important concepts of metaphysical studies. This book is not meant to be a complete anthology of metaphysical thought, but rather an introductory guidebook to the subject. Hopefully it will provide the beginner with a foundation of understandable information upon which to build further, more specific study.

CHAPTER 3

BASIC UNIVERSAL LAWS

UNIVERSAL LAW, WHAT IS IT?

Everyday you work with the laws of nature. Water freezes to make the ice cubes for your drink, fire transforms the log of wood in your fireplace into heat to warm you, and gravity keeps your feet firmly planted on Mother Earth. However, you may not be aware of the set of laws which govern your life (and all of the universe) on the mental/psychological level. Metaphysics terms these laws Universal and they came into being at the same time as natural law. Like natural law, they cannot be overruled. Although you can ignore the Universal Laws, they will function anyway. It is to your benefit to become aware of them and use these Laws to better your life.

Universal Laws do not produce an immediate physical reaction as natural law does, but it will eventually manifest into the physical world. The Universal Laws are more akin to forces that work through your mind and psychological states. While these forces are in operation continuously, your awareness of this process gives you much more balance in daily life, accelerates your spiritual growth and keeps you healthier.

As you become aware of the Universal Laws, you can monitor your thoughts, speech and actions to think in a positive frame of mind, to speak with confidence that you are divinely guided and to act in a manner of unconditional love for all of nature and humanity. This is how you "work" the Universal Laws, by watching and changing your thought and speech patterns and reactions to life situations.

Here is a basic list of Universal Laws and their definitions:

LAW OF ONE

You are one with the Deity, as is all of humanity, whatever you perceive the Deity to be. There is only one Deity, but It is expressed in many different ways, in many different religions, and called by many different names. This One expresses through Nature, through your physical body and mind, and through the various forms of human expression such as art, dance, music, gardening, sexuality, religion and all that is done on Earth.

You can never be separated from this one Deity, although you can deny It, or ignore It, or do things that seem to be un-divine. But you are still one with the One, even at your worst moments. That is why it was said by the Masters, "Everything is one with everything else." All that is on Earth is an expression of the One Deity and is permeated with Its energies. If this were not true, nothing would exist. The energies of the One keeps the universe in motion.

LAW OF MIND

According to metaphysical teaching, when Creation took place it was done through the process of thought, also called the "Mind of the Deity." In the Christian Holy Bible, this is called the "Word of God." Words are the physical manifestation of thoughts, and produce a vibration as does thinking. Therefore by metaphysical interpretation, when the one Deity, which is a vast, unknown void of energy to the finite human mind, began to create the worlds, it was done through vibration. The Bible calls that vibration, or setting atoms into motion to create, a "word." Metaphysics calls it "thought." It is the same concept--a vibratory rate beginning the creation process.

The Law of Mind means that there exists a Universal Intelligence, which is a substance without form. Metaphysics calls this substance the subconscious mind, or the Universal Subconscious Mind. The universal mind substance is also called "the Mind of God." You share this mind substance with the Deity and all other creatures. The purpose of the mind substance is for you to co-create with the Creator. You do this by impressing it with thought images, which if impressed strongly enough with your desires and well-formed visualizations, will manifest into physical form. The Universal Mind Substance is a gift to you from the Deity to allow you to create what you need and desire.

LAW OF LOVE

One of the greatest Universal Laws is the Law of Love. This term means unconditional love for all beings and all things.   Ancient metaphysical texts say that the Deity created out of love.   Pure love is not the emotional response we think of, but is a need to share, to communicate and to give of itself to others. Based on this definition of love, you can see why the Deity is called "A Being of Love." It desires to share, to communicate and to give Its energy to each and every thing on every plane of existence.

Part of this Law of Love includes the love of your Self. This means your personality self and your Higher Self; for both are important. Self-love is not a negative, selfish concept. It is the basis of self-esteem and vital to have before one can love another. Your Higher Self is the Divine Spark within you, but it has to work through your personality self to experience and grow. So any self-condemnation, unnecessary self-denial or rejection of the physical world, is an act against your divine nature. While practical self-discipline is always in order, many of the practices of world religions down through history were extremes of self-condemnation and rejection of the physical plane which the Deity gave to us.

LAW OF DUALITY

Sometimes called Bi-Polarity, this Law basically says that everything has both negative and positive energy within it, including you. This same concept is expressed in the Yin-Yang of the Chinese and the feminine-masculine of the physical body.

According to the Law of Reincarnation, you manifest into either a female or male body each incarnation for the purpose of experiencing the energies of that particular body type. You will eventually learn to master both the feminine and masculine energies of a body. At the same time that you may be living in a female body, you have within you the masculine energies; while your male companion has within him the female energies. Animals, plants, minerals and all things have both the negative-receptive-female force and the positive-active-male force within them.

Taken to a more esoteric level of understanding, the Law of Duality means that the Deity has within It the feminine-masculine energies. That is why you will see in some religions the Deity referred to as Goddess/God or Mother/Father God. This Law of Duality is recognized by all world and earth religions in one form or another.

LAW OF KARMA

As defined in the terminology section, this is the law of cause and effect. Just as in physics where there is an action for every equal and opposite reaction, so is there a cause for every situation in your daily life. Some metaphysical texts call it the "Law of Retribution," but it is not a negative law, for it also brings forth good when you do helpful, thoughtful things for others.

Karma is made by every thought, word and deed, both positive and negative. Based on what you think, do and say, karma is a continuous cycle of energy--mental, emotional and physical that comes back to you in the same way you sent it forth. For example, if you project unconditional love to someone, you will receive the same, and if you feel resentment towards something or someone, you will receive resentment in your life. If you help another, then you will receive help when you need it.

Destiny is what you create for yourself step by step from birth to death. Your destiny is guided by your Higher Self who instructs you along your personal spiritual path. According to the Law of Karma, you will reap what you sow from this lifetime as well as past lives. No one or no thing can exist in the physical world without producing karma. Thus, the best way to live within the Law of Karma is to learn a deeper understanding of your personal self and Spiritual Self so that you can *respond* directly to causes, and not react to effects. Although many have called this the "positive thinking" attitude, I would say it is more on the basis of Positive Living!

LAW OF REINCARNATION

This law goes hand in hand with the Law of Karma, and they are sometimes referred to as "twin laws." Karma keeps us coming back to learn lessons not understood in former lives. Reincarnation gives us the tool to free ourselves from all karma. It is based on the esoteric philosophy that no one has spiritual privileges or gifts except those that have been earned through personal effort throughout a long series of incarnations.

The basic premise of reincarnation is that the human soul lives many lives. With each life, it assumes a new body. This body may be either male or female, depending on what the soul has to experience and learn. As the soul moves from life to life, it gathers experience and evolves to a more advanced human level. The soul acts as a computer storing experiences and feeding the essence of these life experiences back to the Higher Self.

The Higher Self works through the soul, which in turn uses the physical body to learn to conquer the material plane. Thus, your Higher Self has a vehicle through which to learn, since it does not have a physical body.

Reincarnation is not fatalistic, for every individual has free will, as mentioned earlier. The concepts of reincarnation and karma are based on the belief that you are totally responsible for your life situation, past, present,

and future. Nothing outside of you and your free will
determines your situation. You determine it through every
thought, word, and deed. Since you have free will, you
have the power of choice.

Reincarnationists believe that you choose the time period
of your birth, your parents, their financial circumstances,
genetic strengths and weaknesses, race, religion, and area
of the world. Such choices are based on the karma you
have accumulated, both positive and negative, and the
lessons you need to learn. Your family situation will be a
reflection of what you have learned and not learned in past
lives.

Reincarnation gives you an opportunity many times,
through many lives, to grow spiritually and eventually
evolve back to the Deity. It was there, with the Deity, that
you began as a soul.

Why do you evolve back to where you started if you
were a perfect soul in the first place? Metaphysical
teachings relate that, although you were a perfect soul in
the beginning of creation, you and all the other souls were
without experience. Without experience, or a point of
reference, you cannot grow and develop. Earth life offers
the best vehicle for growth, because it has the most
friction. Friction is not a bad thing when it produces
action and progress. You do learn a great deal from
situations that have friction between personalities, or
friction caused by a machine you are learning to operate.

As you learn to overcome difficulties, or friction, you
become a stronger, more productive and self-confident

individual. When you return or evolve back to the Deity, you will bring these qualities of strength, productivity, and self-confidence to the Deity. You are a small part of the Divinity expressed by the Higher Self within you. When you grow spiritually, you help the Deity to grow and expand, for It is not static, but ever-evolving.

Reincarnation and karma working together explains the suffering in the world. For example, if an individual was cruel to another in a former life, that individual may come back in a physically impaired body, or be born to a set of cruel parents so that he may make restitution for his abuse of the other.

Remember, karma is not always negative. If you have been very poor in a former life, but did all you could to lead a moral life, and were kind to others, you may choose to be born into a wealthy family in your next life.

It is important to remember that all you do, say, and think has an impact on your personal life, as well as on the lives of those around you. The more effort you put into monitoring your thoughts, words, and actions so that they reflect the very best within you, the better your life will be and the less struggling you will experience. That does not mean, however, that you will not have to struggle or suffer as you work to express the best within you.

Everything you do requires a period of time to show results, and self-growth is no different. eventually, you do grow to a point where you learn how to respond more objectively to those events outside of your control, such as the actions of others, or the death of a friend.

As you grow, you begin to see that others are walking their personal spiritual paths, and they are responsible for their own actions. If you are doing the best you can by keeping your thoughts, words, and actions pure, and someone does something that seems thoughtless, or vicious to you, you will recover quickly and not suffer harm. This is because you are working in harmony with yourself, your environment, and the Universal Laws.

You are not only going to experience more happiness in the present life, but you are also creating a future life of happiness for yourself. You are now putting for the effort to express the best within you.

ASCENDED MASTERS

When you have conquered the Earth plane frictions and learned to handle all the energies here, including your own energies of both the male and female bodies, you cease to create karma. You become an enlightened soul that chooses whether or not to incarn. Such a soul is called an Ascended Master and will help humanity evolve in spirituality by incarning as a Teacher of Spiritual Truths, or by working from the interdimensional levels.

An Ascended Master is a soul who has "mastered" all there is to learn about the Earth plane, the physical body, the intellect, the emotions, and the subconscious mind, called the etheric/memory body. This soul is finished with the wheel of karma, and does not have to incarn in physical form again. A Master Teacher, such as Jesus, Buddha,

Krishna, and many others, has learned to balance karma
and the energies of the Earth through many lifetimes.
After Mastership is attained, you cease creating karma; all
is within perfect check and balance.

TRANSMIGRATION

A term often used for reincarnation is "transmigration,"
meaning incarnation of a human soul into an animal, insect,
etc. You will find a lot of discrepancy among metaphysical
texts on this subject; however, basically reincarnation
refers to the human soul incarning into human form.
Transmigration is an issue of disagreement among many
metaphysical teachers.

For the purposes of this text, it is understood that the
human soul incarns into a human body. However, the
human soul has experienced, and continues to experience,
many levels of consciousness. One metaphysical concept
is that the soul works through seven stages of
consciousness for experience in the Earth plane: Mineral
consciousness, which is learning to be in the physical form.
Plant consciousness, which is learning to express emotion.
Animal consciousness, which is learning the subconscious
mind. Animal-man, which is learning to use the powers of
the intellect. Human-man, which is combining these four
consciousness states, called the four lower bodies, into a
physical body vehicle to use for a variety of learning
experiences. Presently humanity is evolving into the

consciousness of Intuitive-Man. The stage beyond that is Divine-Man.

Each stage lasts for thousands of years before evolving into the next. Intuitive-Man represents the uniting of the logical mind with the intuitive mind. Humanity will be balancing the extreme reactions of the emotional and mental bodies, and learning to work more intuitively. Eventually we will be more telepathic, able to use our natural healing energies, and not continuously ruled by our emotions or intellect.

LAW OF ATTRACTION

Through your conscious and subconscious thoughts you attract and/or repel people, situations, problems and things. Your mental attitude is the key to controlling the Law of Attraction. If your attitude is one of preoccupation with material things, then materialistic people and situations will be drawn to you. This, of course, is not negative when you need to be involved in the material world. If you are trying to find people of like mind, who are spiritually oriented, then you will have to focus on the spiritual purpose behind the material world. If you are in a positive, uplifting mood, you will attract people and situations that are thoughtful and helpful. If you are in a negative, depressed mood, then you will attract grumpy, self-centered people and frustrating situations.

Your thoughts go out into the Universal Subconscious Mind and attract similar thoughts that give more power to your original thought. As your thoughts attract more and more similar thoughts, they have to manifest eventually into your environment.

Like all the Universal Laws, this Law works negatively or positively. If you are constantly fearful of something, you give it energy through your thoughts and run the risk of attracting it. This is not to say you should not have a healthy caution towards some things, such as walking inner city streets at night or making certain you have substantial locks on doors. However, caution is far different from fear. Caution is respecting the signs of the times in which we live, but fear is demonstrated by those who heavily arm themselves, put up electric fences and post guard dogs.

Becoming aware of this Law does not mean you should walk around doing affirmations struggling to think positively on a continual basis, and leave your door unlocked to prove you are living a positive life! It does mean you can monitor your thoughts to replace negative attitudes with those of self-confidence, reasonable caution and self-esteem.

The implication of this law is that you were to meant to be unhappy or frustrated, and it is your thoughts about yourself, others, and your life that make you miserable. You have free will and you can change your thoughts, and therefore your attitudes, about yourself and others to attract all the good you deserve.

Keep in mind that this law does not mean that you will not have to work at changing your thinking. You will not wake up one morning and decide your attitude is changed

so your life can now flow. You have to work day-by-day
moment-by moment to change your perceptions of things,
and that means becoming aware of your subconscious
thought processes as well. You may decide to use
psychology, counseling, nutrition, or the study of
metaphysics to help you make all these mental changes,
and you will always have to replace a negative attitude with
a positive one.

LAW OF RETURN

Sometimes also called "Law of Circulation" or "Law of
Giving and Receiving." You always have to give to
receive and that means emotionally and mentally as well as
physically. If you cannot give compliments and love to
others, you will not receive them because you have not sent
any energy forth or opened a channel to receive. The
existence of this Law assures you that as much as you give,
you will also receive and often many times over that.
However, just like the Law of Attraction, this works on the
negative as well as positive level. Be careful when you
give out, or hold back, for it just may be that you will need
some of the very thing you withheld.

The Law of Return applies to money, services, thoughts,
words, actions and emotions. On the material side, you
can see this Law working daily in marketing practices.
Companies know that the amount of money, time and
energy spent on advertising determines how their products
sell. The time, effort and money put into something will

circulate back to you just as it was sent out. Sent out with self-confidence, honest, and sincerity, it must come back to you the same way. Send out a shoddy product and watch the number of law suits, dishonest employees and eventual bankruptcy that find its way home to that company.

On the other hand, if you give of yourself by performing a service to another, such as driving an older person to a doctor's appointment or picking up her groceries, you will receive help when you need it. Another example is if you give a donation of $25 to a needy individual or helpful organization, you can expect to receive at least that back, if not more, in services you need or actual money. The Law of Return is also called by some "The Law of Tenfold Return," with the belief that you receive ten times over what you give out. The primary concern should always be the *motive* behind the giving. If it is done unconditionally, without resentment or expectation of a returned favor, it will come back to you in the same spirit.

THE LAW OF FREEDOM

This law could also be called "The Law of Free Will." Each soul, whether it is incarned on Earth or not, has been given the great gift of free will by the Deity. This gift can *never* be taken away from a soul. Free will is an equal and absolute concept.

This law helps to explain why some souls, who appear to be leading wretched and miserable lives, can actually be happy. Making the best of their environment and situation, they have chosen to look at the good things they have and not dwell on what is lacking in their lives.

Free will gives each soul the opportunity to follow its path, to stray from the path, to be happy, or to be miserable. Without the gift of free will, we would merely be robots, following our lives without challenges to test us emotionally, physically, and spiritually. Free will could be seen as the spice we add to life.

CONCLUSION

The importance of Universal Law is that as you become aware of its existence, you can make conscious choices that work within these laws and receive life's continuous flow of abundance. With this basic working knowledge of Universal Law, you can see the usefulness of monitoring your thoughts, words and deeds so that you can receive life's abundance in a continuous flow. The attitudes that block the positive flow of Universal Law and turn the tide of negativity toward you are resentment, fear, anger, greed, jealously, and all negative emotions. They are the greatest wall to your happiness.

SUGGESTED EXERCISES:

1. Now that you are aware of some of the basic principles of metaphysical thought and the Universal Laws, you might keep a notebook or journal of events in your life and how

these coincide with your moods and attitudes. For example, if on Monday through Thursday you were annoyed with a family member and your car stalled one day, someone else got the parking place you circled three times to get, your washer overflowed, and your word processor died, you might want to look at the anger or resentment toward that family member a little closer!

In this exaggerated example of a life situation, it is obvious that the Law of Attraction is working in a very negative manner for this individual. To bring that Law into a positive mode in your life, first try working out the problem with the family member. If that does not succeed, get some counseling for yourself so that you can cope without hostile thoughts toward that individual.

Set up your notebook or journal like this:

Date	Mood/Attitude	Pos. Events	Neg. Events

Take a few minutes before bed to record what went on through the day that were both positive and negative. Record both because you will begin to see, over a period of time, that one outweighs the other according to your mood or attitude.

2. Another exercise that might be helpful is keeping track
of the Law of Return. To do this exercise, set up another
part of your notebook to record the date, the service or
amount of donation given, and then add a column for the
return.   This can be a needed service to you, or
unexpected money, such as a debt repaid, etc.

Date   Service   Donation   Return

CHAPTER 4

RELIGION AND METAPHYSICS

WHERE IS GOD IN METAPHYSICS?

Many people who read about metaphysical subjects ask "Where is God in all this?" There is a mistaken perception that metaphysics is purely intellectual and excludes a Divine Deity. That is unfortunate, because metaphysical study actually expands the concept of God. This can be a problem for new students. When limitations about God are removed, students are asked to open their minds and see the Deity from their own perspective. What you have been told about a Divine Presence by your minister, priest, rabbi or parents may no longer fit your belief system because dogma and doctrine are removed.

Before, God was an externalized Being living in "Heaven," or One Who hurled problems in your path whenever He chose, or was an invisible Being who moved around you and your affairs waiting to intervene when "He" pleased. Now, through the study of metaphysics, you will begin to see a God who makes you an equal, a divine co-creator. You will also be able to remove the strict patriarchal position of the Deity and see there is also a Feminine Principle in God. It is comfortable to most people to have limitations and know exactly how to relate to the Unseen. Unfortunately in most cases that relationship is based on fear, or guilt, depending on how things are going in your life.

In metaphysical study, the place of the Deity is in all things. There is a little piece of the Divine living in all creatures, in all humanity and even in those things called inanimate objects. The teaching is that the Divine Energies are flowing down into you and all things continuously, sustaining everything on Earth. The Deity is not seen as a static entity, but One that is growing and expanding as humanity evolves.

This concept does not negate the belief that the Deity is omnipotent or omnipresent, but it does remove any limitation from God as a being that remains the same. Because humanity is a very large part of God, and humanity is constantly evolving, it seems logical that God must also be evolving. Remember the concept that humanity started as souls without experience, and as it evolves by gathering experience on Earth, so God evolves when the soul returns to the Deity with its vast Earth experience.

YOUR PERSONAL BELIEF SYSTEM

There is no need to change your religion or give up religion because you are studying about God from a new perspective. It is true, however, that once you begin to think of God from a more expanded consciousness, you may change the way you think about religion. The metaphysical perception of God is that It is a good and loving Being. It possesses both male and female energies, just as the soul has both male and female energies within it.

Through the gifts of free will, creative thinking and communication with God through meditation and prayer, God has made you an equal. According to metaphysical thought, the steps in the evolution of humanity eventually lead to what could be termed "Divine-Man." This is a race of humans who can heal at will, and communicate telepathically with each other as well as the nature and angelic kingdoms. Divine-Man looks like a god-being to us from today's point in evolution.

DEFINITION OF RELIGION

The greatest problem for new students when it comes to religion and metaphysics is their definition of religion. Religion is most often considered to be a conglomeration of churches, dogma and doctrine. Webster's defines religion as: "a cause, a principle, or system of beliefs held

to with ardor and faith[1]." Religion can also be defined as
a vehicle for your spiritual search.

Based on the above definitions, neither of which make
any reference to a Deity, any belief system to which you
persistently adhere with enthusiasm and trust can be
classified as a religion. New paths of religion are then
opened to us. Science, philosophy, medicine, the arts,
theology and psychology can be classified as forms of
religion. Certainly people in those fields hold firmly to
their belief systems with "ardor and faith," or they would
not have educated themselves in such studies.

It is unfortunate that we think of religion as church,
priests or ministers, a holy book, and ritual. Anything
outside of these trappings is seen as non-religious and
somehow does not acknowledge a Deity. Through this
analysis of religion, you can see how limiting religion can
become if it is perceived as only the rites of church and
doctrine.

Metaphysics is not a religion. The whole idea of
studying metaphysics is to expand consciousness, not place
limits on it. The ability to shed limitations in thinking
should apply to all aspects of life and not just to religion.
For example, Emily, a student in one of our basic
metaphysics classes, felt that she was a "victim of
circumstances" in her personal relationships with men,
since these never seemed to work for her. When she began

[1]Webster's New Collegiate Dictionary, 1974 edition

exploring her attitudes toward personal relationships with men, she discovered that she looked for either security or a father image. However, a few months into the relationship, she resented the smothering or possessive attitude the man expressed toward her. She realized that deep within she was an independent woman, but she had a difficult relationship with her father and subconsciously continued to look for a father in the men she dated.

Once she learned about the Law of Attraction and understood that because of this subconscious attitude about men she was attracting the wrong kind to her, she began to understand the power of unconscious, false messages that created this attitude. Through conscientious therapy, and her own understanding of Universal Law, she was eventually able to live from an independent nature rather than a dependent one. The men she attracted into her life after this were much more fulfilling to her true nature.

"SATAN" AS A PERSONIFICATION OF NEGATIVITY

The concept of a "Satan," or "devil," as a personified individual simply does **NOT** exist in metaphysics. However, negative energy, which such a creature symbolizes, does exist. It is seen as a product of the lower nature, or dark side of the human personality, the ego which is focused on the five physical senses, the emotions, and the intellect. To understand negative energy, which the terms "Satan" and "devil" personify, you must analyze the terms.

The word "Satan" is a derivative of the word Saturn, which in astrology is the planet associated with the taskmaster, hard work and the struggle to overcome the lower nature. The planet Saturn produces the energies that harden, solidify and create, such as Earth was created by solidification. Satan, rather Saturn energy, then becomes a symbol of that which draws in to make things solid. This is not evil when something is being created.

The term "devil" is a translation from the Latin "daemon" meaning a spirit. In Greek it is "daimon, meaning divine power, fate, or god, and in Greek Mythology was considered a secondary divinity between the gods and mankind. Theologians translated it into the "devil" making it an evil spirit representing the negativity in the world. A further interpretation of "Satan" was from the religious cosmology of a war between the angels, and "Satan" became "Lucifer" who is the fallen angel in theology. "Lucifer" and "Satan" were then referred to as the same being. "Lucifer" actually means "Light-Bearer", however in theology he is the angel who gives up the Light for the darkness of pride and power.

The energies of "Lucifer and Satan" principles are always in conflict, and represent the conflict within each human. This is the conflict between the will to do good, to rise above negativity through identification with the spiritual, Higher Self, and the urge to gratify only the five senses, emotions, or intellect of the individual.

"Satan and Lucifer" energies combined become the "devil" of religion that is personified as an evil being. In further analysis, the "devil" represents the misuse of energies within you and the struggle of light and dark forces of human nature.

Religion personified these energies and called them a "devil" because it needed a dark force to pit against the positive force. In most world religions there is an evil and a good force always working against each other, vying for individual attention. Such a concept is personifying the energies within us of the Higher (Divine) Self and lower self, the personality.

Metaphysics interprets the "devil" of religion as qualities of selfishness, abuse of power, and the excesses within each individual. The role of metaphysics is to guide you to overcome this lower nature, and integrate it with your positive qualities of forgiveness, unconditional love, and service to humanity.

HEAVEN AND HELL

Another important concept in religion is that of heaven and hell. The metaphysical interpretation of heaven and hell is not a place, but rather a state of mind. While there are planes of experience, that might be interpreted as the "heavens" mentioned in the Bible, the word heaven can also mean a positive, loving attitude. An attitude of positive, optimistic thinking, if held long enough, can make the individual live in a "heaven on Earth." Through the

Law of Attraction and this positive state of mind, many good things come to someone who can maintain this mental condition.

If heaven is a state of mind, so is hell. When you think about the negatives in your life and dwell upon lack, you create a living hell for yourself. Again, through the ever-present Law of Attraction, negative thoughts, words and deeds will bring you the worst possible situations. Hell is being surrounded by the demon-like thought forms you create with your own negative thinking. These ugly thoughts twist your perception of life and become your "devil."

Susan, a young mother of two children, who was also a single parent, worked as a secretary for a small business. She could barely meet her rent payment some months, and a movie or dinner out were luxuries. Her former husband was an alcoholic, had been abusive to her and the children, so she was healing from psychological trauma as well as the cold reality of financial struggle. Yet this courageous young woman refused to give up her dream of getting a college education. Susan took night classes swapping baby-sitting with other young mothers. Eventually she was hired by an accounting firm where she worked her way into an executive secretarial position. The firm was so impressed by her persistence and ability with accounting that they now pay for much of her college, even allowing her time off for some day classes.

In sharp contrast to this woman's refusal to make a "hell" out of her life, George, a young man, whose parents were willing to pay for his education, could not decide "what he wanted to be when he grew up." At age 23 he still lived at home, hopped from job to job and used most of his wages to buy drugs. The excuse he used for his behavior was that he was depressed all the time and suicidal.

Here you have an example of two people who make a heaven and a hell of their lives. Susan refuses to accept defeat in the face of consistent adversity, and George cannot lift himself from his self-pity and additive behavior long enough to realize that he is creating his own "hell."

Death is not necessary to experience heaven or hell. Because you have free will, you can choose a positive or negative state of mind. Obviously, it is not easy to change a state of mind. It requires constant monitoring and adjusting of thoughts, words and deeds. The point is that it is possible. It can be done. It is well worth the effort to change a private hell into a personal heaven.

THE PSYCHIC MIND AS A SPIRITUAL GIFT

Another conflict between religion and metaphysics is the idea of spiritual gifts of the psychic mind. Many people have a natural tendency to clairvoyance, clairaudience (see glossary), and the power to heal through their hands and minds. While these spiritual gifts can be abused and become the work of the dark side of human nature when used to manipulate others, or to obtain money,

metaphysical texts teach that psychic abilities, used properly, are gifts from the Divine Presence within each
person.   All   humanity   is   "psychic,"   though   some
individuals are more sensitive to their psychic mind than
others.

If you deny the spiritual gifts of the psychic mind as
"works of the devil" rather than "gifts of God," then you
choose to deny yourself access to information or abilities
that may make your life happier. What greater reference
to the psychic mind as a divine gift can you have than all
the prophets of holy books who talked to God, saw the
future and communicated with angels? How can
something, that has been the natural course of human
events for centuries with positive results, be the "work of
a devil?"

One of these great gifts of sensitivity is the act of
channeling information from other dimensions into the
physical plane. What today is popularly referred to as
"channeling" is a new word for old-fashioned mediumship,
and is actually interdimensional communication.   An
individual bringing information from a dimension other
than the physical plane, acts as a medium for the one
sending the information. Usually the sender is a Being of
Light, such as a Guide, Great Teacher or Angelic
Presence.   Or it may be a Planetarian, a being from a
planet in our solar system or beyond. But, often it is from
the Higher Self within.

Mediumship has been with humanity since the beginning
of time, and in the Bible there are many references to a

prophet acting as a medium for God to speak through. Moses is the best example, as he transcribed the Ten Commandments from communication with the Divine.

Metaphysicians have not done a great deal to reduce the conflict between religion and mediumship, as there is a tendency among them to believe that someone has to be special to be able to channel. The abilities of the psychic mind are not given to those who have received the Deity's special attention, but are innate within all of humanity. It is only the difference in sensitivity to these ever-present abilities of the mental realm that makes one individual a medium, another a clairvoyant, and another a healer. Sensitivity is gradually opened when you study metaphysical material, consciously pursue your spiritual path, and remove the doubt and conflict that blocked your mental potential.

Mediumship, telepathy, clairvoyance and healing are natural gifts that were given to man so that he could be a co-creator with the Deity. This is a very important principle in metaphysics that often conflicts with religion. Religious dogma says that man sins and must suffer for his sins. Metaphysical teachings say that man suffers from his own ignorance and ceases to suffer when he recognizes that he is also Divine and not merely the personality self.

SAVIOR OR MASTER TEACHER?

The essence of this conflict is that most Christian religions teach that mankind has sinned and has to be saved, and that Jesus is the Savior. In order to be "saved," you must confess that Jesus is the Son of God and you are a sinner, who can only be freed by confessing Jesus as your Savior.

The metaphysical interpretation of Jesus is that he is a Great Soul, son of God, and Great Teacher, an Ascended Master, who came to show us a way of life that connects with the Divine within. Metaphysicians teach that we are all sons and daughters of God, because we all have the Divine Spark of God within us. Jesus was an advanced soul, who showed us that we can all become advanced souls. His life was an example of how to do this through unconditional love, service to humanity, and understanding the deep inner meaning of life and God.

By this interpretation of Jesus' work, metaphysicians feel humanity does not need a savior. Each of us is our own savior through the process of coming to know the God-Self within. Both interpretations of Jesus can be correct, if you accept that Christianity is teaching the outer (exoteric) meaning, and metaphysics is teaching the inner (esoteric) meaning of Jesus' life and work.

Another point of friction in religion is around the term "Christ." Christ is a principle, an initiation into a higher consciousness of perfect attunement with the Deity. It is attained by complete devotion to serving humanity and recognition of our true nature as Beings of Light, one with the Deity. Jesus became "The Christ" when he gave up focusing on his personality self and focused entirely on his Divine Presence within. This initiation was also an act whereby he demonstrated to us that we, too, have it within us the power to become "The Christed Principle."

CONCLUSION

The major conflict between metaphysics and religion is that religion teaches through the limitations of strict dogma and doctrine. Metaphysical teachings expand the thought process and encourage investigation. Through the process of questioning, the individual comes to understand the inner meanings of his or her chosen religion.

Metaphysical study does not replace religion, nor should it threaten it. However, if you suffer any doubt about your choice of religion, it will challenge that doubt and force you to examine what it is you believe. There is no authority figure, even in religion, who can tell you what to believe. You have to develop your own belief system through exploration of many different philosophies or world religions. As you go through this process of exploration and questioning, you will eventually find a religion--or belief system--that works for you. That may or may not be the same religious belief you were taught as a child.

In truth, metaphysics and religion are both from the same basic principles. We are a Brotherhood of Man, united through the unconditional love of the One God. Many paths lead to the Deity. Religion and metaphysics are only two.

CHAPTER 5

METAPHYSICAL VIEW OF DEATH
AND IMMORTALITY

YOUR MANY BODIES

In metaphysical teachings death is an extension of life. In fact death is seen as a rebirth into the spirit realm. It is as if you opened a door and, instead of walking into another room, you walk into another dimension. This dimension has people in it, just as our physical world does, except that they have "bodies of Light" rather than physical bodies. The physical body is discarded at death, like outmoded clothing. The form of communication in the spirit realm is telepathy, for mind, or consciousness, lives on.

The physical body is a vehicle through which your soul works to gather experience during your Earth life. The body is a marvelous tool and should be well cared for over the course of your daily living. However, when it is worn out, the soul can be released through the process we call death and go back to the spirit realm to assess its experiences. Remember that experience is the goal of each life for the purpose of evolution. Out of that experience you are to gather understanding and wisdom of your spiritual nature.

According to metaphysical thought, you have more than one body, although you have only one physical body. The other bodies are invisible to the eye and are (1) the etheric body, the one closest to the physical, (2) the astral/emotional body sometimes seen in astral projection, (3) the mental body encompassing abstract and logical thought, and (4) the spiritual body which is very fine in substance and is pure Light. These bodies are invisible because they are of a higher vibration than the physical body, like radio waves or radar. The radiation of all these bodies together make the aura many people see surrounding the physical body.

There are many philosophies, each with its own branch of metaphysics, and each one has a different view of death and the concept of the invisible bodies. Some ancient teachings say there are seven invisible bodies in all; others have as many as twelve. However, for the purpose of keeping this book simple, we will just work with those mentioned above.

WHAT HAPPENS AT DEATH?

Briefly this is what happens at death from the general metaphysical view: (1) The physical body dies when the soul realizes it is no longer able to support life. (2) The soul releases the life force of the individual from the etheric body, the invisible body closest to the physical, and begins moving upward into the next dimension. Several nurses claim to have seen the light blue or white "mist-like" substance of the astral body at the time of a patient's death.

(3) After withdrawing the astral body from the physical body, the soul moves up through the mental and spiritual planes to connect with the Higher Self. At this point, the soul gives its information of the past life experiences to the Higher Self who records these much like a computer. Please realize that we are using a limited, linear type thinking to explain a very abstract process, so understand that this is not as simple, or as physical, as it sounds.

(4) The information recorded from the last life will be integrated with all other past lives of the soul, and will help determine the next life. In other words, when it is time to reincarn, all past life records, including the last life record, will be reviewed. What needs to be learned by that soul is noted so that it can choose an appropriate time period, geographical location, biological parents, and realize its purpose for reincarning.

(5) The soul, once it has completed its task of releasing itself from the physical plane, finally arrives in another dimension where bodies are of pure Light substance.

NEAR DEATH EXPERIENCES

In a near death experience, the person has been clinically dead and brought back to life after a few moments. Some people report going down a long tunnel toward a bright light and meeting a "Being of Light," who is kind and completely non-judgmental. Some report seeing dead relatives and others see an "instant replay" of their lives. These experiences have become more predominate in the last several years. This is probably due to the fact that individuals feel free to report them, and more physicians have taken interest in the reports. Perhaps more than any other incident, the near death experience has proven to those who have trouble accepting an afterlife that one truly does exist in some form.

While no two near death experiences are the same, many have several common elements. All of the people who experienced near death report that death is a dimension of overwhelming peace, love, and knowledge of the universe. More and more the research done on near death experiences takes away the fear of death and gives hope of a positive afterlife.

REINCARNATION OF THE SOUL

Once the soul has deposited its information with the
Higher Self and recorded the essence of the past life, it is
ready for experiences on the inner dimensions.   Many
metaphysical books record the work of souls in
interdimensional temples, schools, or even other planets,
where the soul learns spiritual lessons before reincarning.
Most of these are written through mediumship (channeling)
or from interpretation of ancient metaphysical texts.   For
example, many people are learning about unconditional
love in all its facets, while others are being taught the value
of courage and faith for their next lives.

The time period before reincarnation is open for
discussion as each metaphysical philosophy has its own
view.   Some texts say 50 to 100 years, while others say
several hundred, and still others say it is possible to
reincarn immediately.   There does seem to be agreement
that a soul who reincarns immediately has difficulty in the
new life, since it did not have time to record the essence of
experiences of the last life.   The new personality tends to
have flashbacks of who it was in the former life and may
have difficulty adapting psychologically.   Child prodigies,
such as Mozart or individuals like Leonardo da Vinci, who
was so ahead of his time, are thought to have been souls
who incarned very quickly.

Past life research done by psychologists and physicians
documents many cases of past lives remembered by
children under seven years of age, and by adults under

hypnosis.   Many of these cases of children remembering past lives were reported in India where the concept of reincarnation is well accepted.

Once the soul is ready to reincarn it must review the information from all its past lives to know what is most needed for its growth in the next life. Again, the method of how this is done is open for discussion as different texts say different things.   One major concept is that the soul appears before a council of Higher Beings known as the "Lords of Karma."

This group of Higher Beings guides the soul to see what it needs to learn and what it did not learn in the last life. With their guidance the soul then chooses every facet of its next life, including the gene pool of its future parents. The soul then has a "blue print" of its future life, but not a pre-planned life.   In other words, the soul has free will to choose whatever experiences it desires, negative or positive. All of these choices will be in accordance with the basic blue print of what the soul came to do.

As an example of this concept, let us say you came back to Earth as one of several children in a ghetto family. Your purpose this time around is to learn strength and concern for others. You may make choices that force you into a life of drugs and crime, but this does not negate the blue print. Your soul will continue trying to influence you to go in a more positive direction even when you make negative choices.

Now, you may be so upset by what you see about you in the ghetto experience that you vow to overcome your background and do something of value. Not only that, but you intend to come back (this life) to help the people in this poor neighborhood to better themselves. So you put all your positive energies into becoming a talented athlete, attorney, or social worker. Any one of these choices gives you the opportunity to help others, and you are then right on track with your pre-life blue print.

You may ask "when do we overcome death and stop having to reincarn?" The standard metaphysical answer is "when you learn to balance the excesses in your life and desire to work with the Higher Beings to help humanity evolve." Someone who has learned to do this is referred to as a "Master Soul."

EVOLUTION OF THE SOUL

A Master is one who has gone beyond the cycle of reincarnation by learning to be so balanced in thought, word and deed that he or she does not produce any karma, negative or positive. Such a soul has perhaps spent many lives on Earth refining itself to higher spiritual ideals and balancing excesses within its lives. This Being has earned the right to choose whether or not to reincarn. He or she may stay on the inner dimensions working with other Great Beings to help humanity evolve, or come back to Earth as an "Avatar" which means Master Teacher. Return to Earth is now a matter of choice and not necessity, for the soul has overcome the Law of Cause and Effect (karma) and the friction of Earth life.

The process of overcoming death is learned life after life as the soul develops itself spiritually. Many trials and much suffering may be incurred before the soul is done, but finished it will be at some point in time. That is why it is important to work with a positive perspective about life and be aware of your attitudes and reactions to your present situation.

"Man Know Thyself" was an axiom written over the door of Plato's school. The ancients felt that when you know yourself, you take personal responsibility for every action, word, and deed realizing that you are a Divine Being, too. Only by knowing yourself can you know the Deity.

Several sects of pre-orthodox Christianity called the Gnostics, believed that each individual was destined to experience *"gnosis," or knowledge of God*, without an intermediary such as a priest or guru. Gnosis was a direct contact with the Deity, and the Gnostics believed the individual was enlightened and had overcome negativity. When the individual died, the experience of gnosis was never lost but imprinted on the soul. Therefore death was the end of the life that had given the greatest growth experience, and in the next rebirth that person would come back as a more evolved soul.

The concept of the evolution of the soul often brings up the questions, "do we ever go backwards?" and "do we never learn?" Metaphysical philosophies are very different in their views on these questions. It is the view of the authors that we all eventually learn. It may take many lifetimes and a soul may appear to be going backwards, however the truth is that it is "restricted" to its present understanding, or more specifically misunderstanding. A soul does eventually move forward in evolution, but it may remain stranded in false attitudes of anger, despair, domination or hatred for many lives. At some point, the evolution of humanity will force it to face itself and demand that it make changes. If such a soul still chooses not to grow--all of us have Free Will--it will essentially remain in its self-made darkness until it is awakened by a Master Teacher or other Higher Being. It is our understanding that the situation of that soul is then up to the Deity, working with the Master Teacher, to decide what to do with it.

Metaphysics stresses very strongly that there is immortality and that death is merely a door to other dimensions. This premise cannot be proven by scientific methods. You will have to study and question and test this concept through your own experiences. Then someday, in some life, you too will have "gnosis," and rebirth will be a choice rather than a necessity.

PERSPECTIVE ON UNDERSTANDING DEATH

Many people come to the study of metaphysics with a fervent desire to help humanity, but they have not learned to control their own emotions or personal habits. How can they help others when they have not learned to help themselves?

Another example of one who wants to help but is not ready is the student of metaphysics who thinks he has completed his Earth tasks and is ready to "ascend" beyond the physical plane, whatever that means to him. So, he spends his life separated from other people because they are too materialistic or too "Earthy" for him. He rarely accomplishes anything of value because he is not willing to come down from his "pedestal of ascension" long enough to help the rest of us who are doing our best just to live a good life.

Probably the worst example of a metaphysical student who has come nowhere near understanding or overcoming the death process, is the one who is always ready to leave the physical plane when things are not going well. This person is ever ready to "checkout" because he thinks he knows how to leave his physical body, and worse yet, he actually thinks he is done. Nonsense! He is still in metaphysical kindergarten and is using his limited knowledge of metaphysics to escape real life. Every little illness or setback in his life causes a suicidal reaction. This person was struggling with old issues of ego and self-esteem before he ever started studying metaphysics, and with this attitude has not much improved.

The daily newspapers and television news are filled with violent acts. Did you ever wonder what deep neurosis or behavior pattern prompted an individual to a violent act? While you may blame poverty, ignorance and greed, just as likely the violent pattern was set up in another life when the person was perhaps an Inquisitor killing or torturing the "heretics," a Roman soldier conquering whole cultures of people for Rome, or a medieval knight trained to kill "in the name of the King." This is not to say that poverty, ignorance, and greed, diseases of our society, did not contribute to the individual's actions. However, his soul pain of past lives misspent and misunderstood contribute greatly to his violent acts in the present life.

CONCLUSION:

Death is not a vehicle to escape daily problems, although it is a temporary release from pain and suffering. Whatever you did not complete or learn to do properly in that former life will be presented to you with even more difficulty in the next life. Death or reincarnation is not a way out of personal responsibility. Lessons in living with unconditional love for all, balancing emotions and having a joyous attitude do not just go away because you die. The lessons will be presented over and over again until they are learned, no matter how many times you come back to Earth life.

CHAPTER 6

THE VALUE OF DREAMS

THE PURPOSE OF DREAMING

Each night you have a metaphysical experience referred to as dreaming. Your dreams are a direct link to the metaphysical world because they come to you from the hidden depths of your subconscious mind. As you have learned your subconscious holds all your attitudes, negative and positive, and your personal perception of reality. Dreaming allows your mind to sort out these attitudes and perceptions to relieve the stress built up from daily interactions at work, in relationships or other activities. Dream research has now proven that we have to dream to allow the body and mind to rest. Participants in sleep laboratories, who were consistently awakened just as they reached a level of deep sleep, became disoriented, belligerent and unable to think clearly.

The value dreams have in your metaphysical studies is that they help you resolve internal conflicts that block your personal and spiritual growth. In fact dreams are status reports about your (1) physical, (2) psychological and (3) spiritual conditions. Dreams balance your mind by playing out frustrations, fears, doubts, and anger through dream characters and images. They heal your body by giving messages about what part of your physical body needs attention. For example, automobiles are a dream symbol of your physical body, because your body is the "vehicle" through which your mind and soul work. If in a dream the automobile you are driving all of sudden does not have brakes, your mind is telling you to slow down and give your body a rest. Set some limitations and structure your time better or your auto (physical body) might "crash" through a serious illness.

One-third of your dreams will be precognitive, that is they will tell you about future events. This percentage varies from person to person, of course. Some people have many precognitive dreams while others feel they never dream about future events. Dreams are a valuable tool for charting your spiritual progress. They allow you to understand your life situation on a deep, psychological and spiritual level. Because your awareness is raised to your inner self, due to your study of metaphysical principles, you will be better able to understand dream messages. Not only are your fears, doubts and worries presented to you in dreams, but also your triumphs and future goals.

THE LANGUAGE OF DREAMS

Dreams come to us in a coded language of symbolism. Learning to interpret the symbols is like learning a foreign language, you need some basic understanding and lots of practice. The dream language encompasses two sets of symbolism: (1) universal, based on archetypes and dream research, and (2) your personal symbolism.

Your personal dream symbolism will be recognized as you record and work at interpreting your dreams. Many people underestimate the value of their personal dream symbols thinking that dream books that interpret symbols is more accurate than their own feeling about a symbol. This is a mistake. Your mind will pick and choose from the events, people and places recorded in your subconscious and choose a series of dream symbols that have consistent meaning to you.

For example, when Jane was in her late twenties, she began having a series of dreams about witches. Since she had not studied any of the pagan religions and was living in a very fundamentalist environment at the time, this symbol seemed out of place to her. Upon following the record of the dreams over a time period of one year, she began to realize the symbol of a witch meant to her a great change was coming into her life. Indeed that is exactly what happened as she moved to another state, started college courses, and divorced. In retrospect she realized the symbol of a witch meant to her, at that point in time, someone who changes the shape of things through magic. So her dreams were telling her she was going to reshape her personal life.

C.G. Jung was the psychologist responsible for introducing the concept of archetypes. His interest in a "collective unconscious" where he believed images of mythological characters, religious symbolism, and occult symbols are stored, led him to think of these as archetypes of the race consciousness. This concept is very close to the metaphysical principle of a Universal Subconscious Mind where all thought images of every individual are stored. The archetypes represented the emotions and perceptions of an individual at certain stages of life, such as youth, the householder stage of spouse and family, old age and wisdom, and the search for spirituality.

Consequently Jung's research into the Eastern philosophies and his interest in dream symbolism as a means to understand psychological problems, produced a wealth of information about archetypes and their meaning and importance in dreams. His theory of dream interpretation is that every thing and every one in the dream is part of the dreamer. The dream characters and dream images represent attitudes and reactions to waking life situations, both negative and positive.

FLYING AND FALLING

In a dream flying represents your feeling that you are overcoming a situation. You are literally "rising above the circumstances." It also is a symbol that you are astral projecting, meaning that you are having an out of body experience. Astral projection means that your physical body is at rest while you are "out" traveling about in your astral body. Flying is a symbol of that experience, although many metaphysical texts on dreams say that we astral project each night as we fall asleep. The purpose of astral projection is that it is necessary to leave the physical body to allow it to heal and release the stress of the day.

Falling is also related to astral projection in that it is a symbol of coming back into body. It is a myth that you will die if you land in the dream. We have landed many times and we are here to write this book! The deeper meaning of falling is that you feel out of control in a life situation, or that you are falling out of balance with a particular part of your life.

LUCID DREAMING

If you are dreaming and suddenly find yourself thinking, "this is a dream," you are experiencing a lucid dream. You are aware while in the dream state that you are dreaming, and because of this awareness you are able to control the dream. There are many dream books on the market that teach techniques to learn lucid dreaming. The idea behind these methods is that if you can have lucid dreams at will, you are able to control your waking life situations more effectively. Lucid dreaming is thought to be a symbol of taking power over your own life and putting it in the direction you desire it to go, rather than being swayed by others' opinions.

Learning to take control of your dream characters while you are dreaming, and making them do what you desire, strengthens your personal willpower. For most people lucid dreams come only occasionally, but dream researchers believe that you can train yourself to dream lucidly. Spiritually the purpose of learning lucid dreaming is to integrate your conscious (waking life) mind with your subconscious mind. When these two parts of your mind are working together, they open the door to the superconscious mind where your Higher Self rules.

The Higher Self is then able to communicate more directly with the conscious mind. Since the very essence of metaphysical principles is to awaken the conscious mind to the spiritual plane, you can see how important the contact with your Higher Self is. Lucid dreaming helps this process, however so does the practice of meditation, visualization, concentration, and ritual.

REMEMBERING YOUR DREAMS

Many people feel they do not dream. However, as mentioned above, everyone dreams because dreaming is necessary to balance and heal the mind and body. What these people are experiencing is inability to remember their dreams. When you begin to read about dreaming and study methods of dream interpretation, your consciousness is raised to the importance of dreams and it becomes easier to remember your dreams.

Techniques to encourage this remembrance include putting a small notebook, or journal, by your bedside. Each night before you drop off to sleep tell yourself: "I will remember my dreams." Mentally repeat this phrase over and over. After about a week, if not much sooner, you will begin to remember fragments of your dreams or whole dream scenes. You might even find yourself awakening right after a dream session. This is usually temporary and will pass as you become more confident in your ability to remember your dreams upon awakening. Eventually your subconscious mind will realize, through your programming it with journalizing and studying dreams, that you *want* to remember your dreams.

As you awaken and begin to remember your dreams, write down the "feeling" of the dream. Did you feel frightened, angry, happy, or confused in the dream? The feelings produced by the dream events will give you some indication of what your mind is trying to tell you about what is really happening in your waking life. You may think you are aware of your life situations, but your subconscious mind often has a far different view of these.

Sometimes you might awaken with only a sense of colors or images left over from your dreams. Write these down in your dream journal along with the feeling of the dream. Even if there is not enough information to interpret the dream, the action of writing down what you did recall reinforces to your subconscious that you want to remember your dreams.   As you write down future dreams the remnants of these past dreams may trigger a recall of them. You may also find the colors and feelings of the past dreams fit into the interpretation of recent dreams.

INTERPRETING YOUR DREAMS

While there are many dream interpretation books on the market, and you will have to choose the method that works for you, there are some basic rules to get you started interpreting your dreams. Always record your dreams as if you are experiencing them now. Do not say "I was doing," say "I am doing..." This helps you to recall more of the dream and to relive the feelings of the dream, which is very important to its interpretation.

Give your dreams a title and make it a very literal one. An example of a title for Jane's dreams about witches could be, "I Am Watching Witches." Basic, but to the point enough that when she looks back into her dream journal for correspondences with other dreams, she can find that particular dream on witches easily.

Interpret from the viewpoint that everything and every person in the dream is a part of yourself. What does antique furniture represent? Old, outworn ideas to be discarded, or priceless advice from an older person? Look at the people in your dream and if you recognize them, see what attitude that person holds that you also have. Perhaps the individual has the complete opposite attitudes about life that you have. In that case, look for what that individual believes that most irritates you. This will be what your mind is telling you to be aware of and correct within yourself. Is it intolerance, prejudice, egotism, fear, passivity? Any of these things can be a part of your own problem to work on, and not always an indication that you dislike that person.

All dreams are interpreted on many different levels. For an easy method of interpretation, look for three levels: 1) physical, i.e. health or problems in job or relationships and of which you are aware in waking life; 2) mental, your psychological state about your life situations; and 3) spiritual, your Higher Self telling you where you are on your Spiritual Path. Here is an easy way to set up your dream journal to help you in dream interpretation:

Date Day of week   Moon Phase (full, waxing, waning, new)

Title of the Dream

Write out the dream(s) using first person and recording feelings, colors, images, numbers, everything you can remember.

INTERPRETATION:
What is going on in my life at the present time?
Record all the work situations, relationship problems, on going spiritual studies, religious activities, etc. Particularly list any personal or health problems you are experiencing now.

PHYSICAL: Here list the symbols that seem to involve your physical body, job situation, or relationship problem and what you think or feel they mean.

MENTAL/EMOTIONAL: Here list the feelings about the dream, and the attitudes or fears you think the dream characters or images represent.

SPIRITUAL: Write down the spiritual message you think is coming through this dream. This will probably be your most difficult part of the interpretation, but persist in looking for the spiritual part of the dream for it is there. If you are doing regular meditation, spiritual or religious study, or if you just started a new self-discipline of some kind, a spiritual message is definitely going to be in the dream.

After you have completed this recording of the dream, you can then look back over a week of dreams and see if there is any recurring symbolism. If not, look over a month's dreams, etc. The idea is to find your personal dream symbolism, and look for a personal conflict or attitude of which you may not be aware. Your dreams are telling you everything you need to balance your life, but you are the only one who can realize what the dreams are saying. Dreams are messages from your Higher Self and subconscious mind to help you stabilize your health, mental state, and spirituality.

BRIEF CHART OF DREAM SYMBOLISM

People: Represent a mirror image of your attitudes and emotions; even if opposite.

Animals: Since animals work out of instinct, they are symbolic of your habits. A rabbit can be passive; a dog obedient, and a tiger aggressive. See what the animal means to you.

Birds: Birds fly high in the air, so they can mean your spiritual self, or spiritual feelings.

Fish: Since the beginning of Christianity, the fish has symbolized spirituality, i.e. the spiritual side of you. Look at the condition of the fish and what you are doing with it or to it.

Plants: Including trees, plants are a symbol of new growth and healing.

Insects: Unless it is a beetle, symbolic of
                    the Ancient Egyptian scarab,
                    insects are habits you wish to
                    discard. However, butterflies are
                    a symbol of rebirth and renewal,
                    and fireflies can mean insight or
                    awakening since they have a
                    light.

Vehicles: Cars, trains, buses, ships, airplanes, all
                    mean vehicles which you use to get
                    things done.   An auto is the most
                    interesting because it also symbolizes
                    your physical body.   Mass transports
                    generally mean corporations, organ-
                    izations, committees, groups, etc.

Houses: The main part of the house is
                    your conscious self, the
                    second floor is your
                    subconscious, and the third
                    floor is your superconscious.
                    The basement is where you
                    store your doubts and fears.
                    Look at the condition of the
                    exterior and rooms, and see
                    if the basement is neat and
                    clean, or cluttered and dirty.

NUMBERS

Numbers in dreams occur in clocks, calendars, telephone numbers, apartment or house numbers, someone telling you a time you are to be somewhere, etc. Use a simple numerology method to find the basic meaning: add all numbers together and if it is a single digit, use the meaning of that number for the interpretation.

If it is a double digit, add the two numbers together until you get one digit. You should acquire a book on numerology to get more detail but here is a simple interpretation of numbers:

1 - The beginning of something.
2 - Peace or contemplation.
3 - Creativity.
4 - Practicality, work.
5 - Change.
6 - Service.
7 - Control.
8 - Power.
9 - Completion.
10 - Specifically completion with a new beginning.

COLORS

Colors in dreams are important because they tell you the emotions of the dream and what level of consciousness you are in. Black and white dreams are a very shallow sleep and usually very physical dreams, or nightmares.

Bright colors are deeper into the subconscious mind and therefore a deeper sleep. Pastels are closer to the superconscious mind, and dreams in all white are in the superconscious and very spiritual.

Pink   - Love, kindness, unconditional concern.
Green   - Healing and growth.
Blue   - Truth.
Gold   - Wisdom.
Silver - Intuitive.
Red   - Activity, leadership, or aggression.
Violet - Royalty, and spirituality
Indigo - Astral planes, formative state
White   - Enlightenment
Black   - Mystery, hidden

Again, you will need to obtain a dream book that deals specifically with colors and numbers to get a more detailed meaning of the significance of each color and number. However, this brief interpretation will get you started thinking about the meaning of numbers and colors in your dreams.

CONCLUSION

Dreams are a very important part of metaphysical study since they reveal your inner most desires, fears, accomplishments and spiritual growth.

In this chapter we have given you the basic structure of dream symbolism and interpretation. We hope that you will refer to the reading list in the back of the book and find books that will help you further in your dream study. This list, too, is brief and we would suggest you go to a metaphysical book store and ask the owner what he or she recommends in the way of dream books. There are many excellent dream books on the market and you need to use your intuitive mind to decide which one is best for you.

CHAPTER 7

TECHNIQUES USED IN THE STUDY OF METAPHYSICS

VALUE OF CONCENTRATION, VISUALIZATION AND MEDITATION

Metaphysical study requires a great ability to concentrate since you are working with abstract thought. It is customary early in metaphysical studies to begin concentration, visualization and meditation techniques. The purpose of these exercises is to teach you to be comfortable working with your mind and to develop one pointed focus.

You can train your mind to become like a laser that beams in on its object and performs whatever duty it was sent forth to do. In the case of metaphysics that duty will be visualization to manifest positive things into the physical world, and calming the mind so that the physical body relaxes.

Meditation exercises provide a twofold purpose. They lower stress and high blood pressure, and they integrate your conscious mind with your superconscious, the Higher Self. This connection between the two minds is similar to the left brain/right brain theory in that, as you learn to connect with your superconscious mind, you tap into creative energies. You also establish communication with your Higher Self. The benefits of meditation and concentration exercises have been touted in many books on sports, self-healing and motivational techniques.

Most new students complain that there is not enough time to do the exercises and occasionally that may be true. However, the majority of new students are sadly lacking in self-discipline. Doing meditation and concentration exercises regularly, along with all the above described benefits, also builds self-discipline and self-esteem. The exercises build self-esteem because when you have the self-discipline to do something well, you feel good about yourself.

As all learning is cumulative and expands into areas other than the focus of study, this self-discipline can be applied to other areas of life. It takes self-discipline to be good at anything: playing an instrument, being on a team, sticking to a tough assignment, operating a business, and managing a household. Building self-esteem and self-discipline encourages personal and spiritual growth.

USING THE TECHNIQUES

Now that you are eager to develop the good habit of self-discipline through doing concentration and meditation exercises, your first assignment will be to create the time to do them. You first have to decide if you are a morning person or a night person. Once you decide this you can schedule your exercises accordingly, by getting up one-half hour early or going to bed one-half hour later. Some people are not able to do this, so they have to place their exercises at intervals during the day. You always have more time than you think, but you do not realize this because you put other activities in these time slots.

For instance, a ride on a train or bus into work can be a place for concentration and meditation. What better environment for learning to focus your mind than while you are surrounded by the dull hum of wheels or low murmur of conversation. The time spent in front of a T.V. can usually be cut considerably, and a lunch hour spent in a park or quiet retreat can be another time spot for concentration, meditation or visualization exercises.

You may be thinking it is impossible to concentrate when other people are making noise all around you. However, you can learn to focus, to concentrate so well that the noise becomes a distant, almost non-existent blur. When this happens you have developed excellent concentration.

Your work-a-day world is the perfect environment to learn and to put into practice your metaphysical learning and studies. This is true whether you are a hard driving executive or a busy young mother.

A CONCENTRATION EXERCISE

Here is an example of a concentration technique that could be practiced anywhere, even while staring out a window of a bus or train. It is called "following your breath:"

Breathe normally, but begin to concentrate on your breath, watching it flow in and out. Notice the breath sounds as you breathe. Do not count your breaths and do not mentally chant anything. Just observe and concentrate on your breathing. As your mind begins to wander, bring it back to observing your breath. Do this for five to ten minutes every day. You can perform this exercise with your eyes closed pretending you are asleep so the chatty guy in the seat next to you will not be tempted to talk to you. Or you can focus on a newspaper, the back of the seat in front of you, or your briefcase, simply using one of these things as a focal point. Pretty soon you will feel as if you are standing inside yourself observing your breath. Some people say they feel as if they are standing inside their nostrils, as if they are inside a giant tunnel.

The idea behind any concentration exercise is to help you become the master of your mind, and not allow it to rule you by wandering. Concentration exercises also develop a

stronger will, which you will need to make the time for
your studies and exercises, and to accomplish your highest
goals in life.

VISUALIZATION

Visualization is a technique of creating mental images of
what you desire in life. Many good books are available on
the use of "creative visualization" to make your life more
abundant, healthier and happier. The basic idea is that you
image, or visualize, what it is you want to manifest into
your physical world. If it is wealth, then you might
visualize a stream of money flowing into your bank account
or wallet. If it is health, then you would see yourself very
healthy and being physically active. You can also visualize
a better attitude, courage, happiness, etc.

Visualization works. A young man with a remodeling
business, who was a student in one of our classes, decided
to try it. For two weeks every time he showered, Tom
visualized filling out a deposit slip for $10,000. After the
two weeks were over, he released the idea by not doing the
visualization.

About one week after his visualizations stopped, a client
came into Tom's office and wrote a check for the exact
amount he had visualized as a down payment on a
remodeling project.

Visualizations must be specific. Another student
visualized himself driving an expensive sports car. He

actually won a car like it in a contest, but had to sell it because he could not afford the insurance, license and gas for a new and expensive sports car!

Visualization works based on the concept of thought forms that are built upon the astral plane when you think. Your thoughts build "thought forms" and these do not just float about your head, then dissipate. Thought forms are created in the lower astral plane of the Universal Subconscious Mind. If given enough thought energy, they must manifest into the physical world. Astral plane substance could be compared to modeling clay as it is somewhat dense, although not as dense as matter on the physical plane. Thoughts are formed from this astral substance immediately, but will usually not manifest unless there is enough emotional desire put into the thought to "push it out" into the physical world.

Your energized thought form attracts other thought forms that "flesh it out," adding energy to it, so that eventually it is developed enough and must come into the physical world. That is why the more you think about something, the more power you give that thought to manifest at some point in time.

As discussed earlier, you do NOT have the right to visualize something that will harm another, or make another do something for you they may not wish to do. For example, you should not visualize a person you would like to love you doing this, as that may not be the best for either of you. That is forcing someone to do something against their will. If that person wants to love you, he or she will, and you do not need visualization techniques to make it happen.

Remember, also, that you are personally responsible and even if you do not acknowledge the concept, you work under Universal Law. So what you create comes back to you threefold and sometimes tenfold. Be very careful what you visualize and *BE PERSONALLY RESPONSIBLE.*

Visualization is used in metaphysical study to help you see that you are not a powerless individual, and that you are creating your world all the time. However, conscious visualization is much more powerful and effective than the unconscious visualization that you used until you became aware of the power of your thoughts.

MEDITATION

Meditation is focusing the mind on one subject, such as a word, symbol, your breath, or a mantra (chant). The body and mind are quiet, listening to your Higher Self within you. Prayer is talking to the Deity and meditation is listening to It.

Many methods of meditation exist, some very passive and others active, involving visualization. The purpose of meditation is primarily to be able to "hear" the inner voice of your Higher Self, but some wonderful side effects come out of meditation practice. The body organs, muscles and nervous system receive a rest during meditation because your thinking is focused, and the body does not have to respond to your scattered thoughts. This is why your blood pressure is lowered during meditation.

You are probably not aware of what a congestion of impulses, tension and nervousness you create by scattered thinking. The mind and the body, because the two are interconnected, are literally pulled in many directions. When you begin to respond out of focused thinking, you become more efficient in your work, less tense, and not angry or upset. This is because you are thinking one thing at a time and doing one thing at a time, with focused attention, rather than juggling four or five different things.

PURPOSE OF METAPHYSICAL EXERCISES

Concentration, visualization, and meditation are all used for one basic purpose, to expand your consciousness. As you become more aware of how your thoughts, words, and actions affect you and those around you, you begin to grow and awaken spiritually. You begin to evolve!

Evolution is why you are on Earth. What is even better than your own evolution is that you then become a Teacher to help others evolve. It is rather like climbing a ladder and reaching down to help another up the ladder. The more that humanity evolves, the more Earth evolves beyond pollution, greed and fear. You truly do have an effect on yourself and everything around you. When you become more aware, you are consciously helping evolution.

CONCLUSION

It sounds so easy, so basic, yet it takes work to live with focused thinking. Would you rather be frustrated, angry and upset or would you like to be calm, focused, and efficient? Being frustrated and angry is easy; anyone can do that. Being calm and focused takes work at first and a willingness to be temporarily uncomfortable, but the rewards are tremendous. It is your choice.

CHAPTER 8

THE PSYCHIC EXPERIENCE
THROUGH
READINGS & TEACHERS

WHAT IS TRUTH?

It is unfortunate that the field of metaphysics has been infiltrated by frauds and charlatans casting a negative light on the entire subject. We recommend that you approach metaphysical information with a sincere desire to learn blended with a healthy skepticism and discriminating attitude. Top notch metaphysical teachers continue to be very discriminating and often skeptical about new information coming into the metaphysical world. This attitude extends to their own channeled material and messages from their Guides. They know nothing should ever be taken as a "Truth" until it passes the judgment of their own intuitive minds and the test of time. After awhile every student exchanges discrimination and skepticism for pure intuition.

The key to weeding out the charlatans of metaphysics is your own intuition; that is, how does the information *feel* to you? Does it open new doors in your mind and make sense to you? When real Truth is spoken or written, you will experience something within yourself that illuminates your inner being. It is as if one thousand bright lights were turned on simultaneously in a dark room.

When you recognize Truth, you understand and see with new vision. The source of the Truth, the religion or philosophy, or belief system does not matter. You will *know* it is a Truth. That is the experience of intuition and recognition of a Truth.

Truth teachings have no boundaries and are not the possession of a privileged few. No one philosophy, religion, or system owns "The Truth." The Deity was wise in distributing pieces of Truth to all religions, cultures, and philosophies so that everyone has the opportunity to find a spiritual path. So if anyone tells you "this is the only way" something can be, or "this is The Truth," be wary and aware that **even if it feels right to you, it still is only a piece of the whole of the Truth Teachings.**

A wise scientist experiments with many different materials before he concludes what works best for his particular experiment. The metaphysical student should be no less wise. Many students ask us "where do I go to find information on metaphysics?" We hope this text will be a good foundation for you, and our reading guide in the back of it should also help. However, a good metaphysical book store or the New Age/Occult/Philosophy/Religion sections of a regular book store are good places to begin your search. Look over the titles and let your intuitive mind take over. Choose what feels right for you at that moment, for undoubtedly your taste will change as you grow in your understanding of metaphysical principles. Since, as we said earlier, metaphysics encompasses parts of psychology, physics, philosophy, theology, holistic health, astrology, and esoteric science, you have quite a wide range of subjects from which to choose.

PSYCHIC FAIRS

Many times throughout the year you may see advertisements for psychic fairs. These events are often set up in a shopping mall, community center, or in a large meeting room of a hotel. Often the psychic fairs are sponsored by a metaphysical book store, or by a group of metaphysical people who do readings, sell crystals, etc. While there is nothing wrong with attending a psychic fair and enjoying the interaction with metaphysically minded individuals, there are things to be wary of. We give you a look at the positive and negative side of psychic fairs.

You want to use your discriminating intuition at the fairs. The atmosphere of a psychic fair is charged with excitement and fun. There are many displays including jewelry of metaphysical symbols, crystals, rare oils, herbs and a number of readers. It is a good place to contact meditation groups, to sign up for metaphysical classes and lectures, and to browse through an excellent selection of books.

However, if there is one event that attracts charlatans, a psychic fair is it. They love the attention showered upon them by those new to metaphysics and can be quite entertaining. Their misinformation unfortunately can also be very harmful psychologically to an oversensitive or gullible individual. Use your intuition actively while at a psychic fair, and remember what we said, "Truth comes in many pieces and not all in one package."

We are not trying to discourage you from attending psychic fairs. They are fun and a good way to make contacts with metaphysical groups and teachers. Just remember that the lower psychic mind is the first step in your awakening to other realms of consciousness, not the entire staircase.

READINGS & WHAT TO LOOK FOR IN A "READER"

1. Does the person doing the reading present him or herself in a professional manner?

2. Will the reader look you directly in the eyes? This may seem like a simple issue, but someone who cannot look you in the eyes is either too shy, or too sly, to be working with psychic energies.

3. No reader should ever tell you that something cannot be changed. You have free will to change anything, including information given you in a reading.

4. A reader should never predict a death or say something is "evil." A death of anyone, or anything, is between that soul and God. That soul may decide to stay around awhile longer, so it is difficult, not to mention highly unethical, to predict death. As far as "evil" goes, any metaphysical reader, or teacher, or a basic student for that matter, knows that evil is misdirected energy which is attracted by fear and dishonesty with self and others. The term a reader should use is "negativity", and then specifically explain where he thinks this originates. Even then you should discern if this "feels" correct to you. Often a reader feeling negativity about you is feeling your personal, negative issues you are, hopefully, working at healing.

5. A reader should charge a reasonable fee, and should never ask for a constant flow of money from you "to protect you from evil," or "return your health," or "bring you love," etc.

6. If the reader is not taping your reading for you, you should always be allowed to tape it yourself.

7. If at any time during the reading you feel very uneasy about what is being said, or the atmosphere is uncomfortable, or anything else about the reader makes you ill at ease, end the reading. Thank the reader for his or her time and express that you do not feel this is right for you at this time. **AND DO NOT PAY ANYTHING.** A good reader will understand and respect your integrity for doing this.

8. Always get a business card or name, address and phone number of the reader so that if you have any questions later, you can call to have these answered. Honest readers will tell you to contact them if you have any questions regarding your reading.

9. You should be able to ask the reader about his or her experience and background in doing readings, study of metaphysical subjects, or whatever (within reason) you desire to know about their ability to do readings.

The psychic mind is a gift from the Deity and ability to do a reading is a tool for self-help and service to others. However, the person using this tool must constantly study and work to remove his or her psychological, emotional, and spiritual blocks.

TYPES OF READINGS

PALMISTRY: You have an imprint of your life on your palm. The lines show the way you think, how close you were to your family as you grew up, how you react in personal relationships, your motivation or lack of it in a job or career, and if you have a material or spiritual attitude toward life. The palm reader works from the intuitive level of mind, and your palm is only a focus for the reader "to tune in" to your subconscious mind.

CRYSTAL SKRYING: The crystal ball is a means of focusing the mind of the reader to be able to attune to your mind and "read" what is in your subconscious.

AURA READING: People who see auras can tell you things about your health and emotions. However, you should always see a qualified physician for diagnosis and treatment of health problems. The reader also uses the aura as a focus to read your mind.

TAROT READING: The Tarot is a deck of 72 cards with symbolic pictures representing the spiritual, psychological and material planes of consciousness. A competent Tarot Reader can be quite helpful in giving you a synopsis of what experiences you are creating in the future, as well as past experiences influencing your life now. The spiritual part of the reading can help you understand where you are on your Spiritual Path. The Tarot is often referred to as "Keys of Wisdom."

THE RUNES: The Runes are similar to the Tarot in that they evolved from ancient cultures and can be used as Keys of Wisdom. They can be useful, as in the Tarot, in helping you understand where you are going so long as you realize you are creating your own situations. Runes are of unknown origin, although they are usually associated with the Scandinavian culture. They are symbolic glyphs carved on pieces of wood or stone. They are interpreted from the Book of Runes.

I CHING: I Ching is considered an ancient Chinese oracle and similar to the Runes, only in Oriental thought. Coins or yarrow sticks are interpreted by the way they fall, using the sayings in the Book of I Ching for interpretation.

AKASHIC RECORDS: Akasha is a higher plane of consciousness, and holds the records of each soul's path from life to life. Akashic Record Readings will reveal psychological blocks developed in this life or past lives, your spiritual roots (which are probably far different from your religious upbringing this life) and tell you where you are on your Spiritual Path. Akashic Readings will also reveal your purpose of the present life. Akashic Readers are fewer in number because of the number of years of intensive training required to learn to read Akasha.

PAST LIFE: Many readers profess to see past lives. Most past life readers are reading the memories you have of your past lives stored in your subconscious. You can easily read these yourself through self-hypnosis techniques designed to access your own past lives. In addition, within the last several years, a new therapy called Past-Life Regression Therapy has developed utilizing hypnosis by a therapist to uncover past life traumas. The theory is that in "reliving past life experiences," through hypnosis, you release pain of the physical body, emotional, and mental bodies of this life.

When working with a past life reader, keep in mind that NO PAST LIFE READER, OR AKASHIC READER SHOULD EVER TELL YOU THAT YOU WERE A VERY FAMOUS PERSON IN HISTORY. While it does happen that a reader uncovers a past life in which the individual was a famous, or infamous, person in history, it is very rare that people who are performing the everyday living patterns of normal human life are reincarnations of historical figures. Just be cautious of such information by discerning within yourself whether or not it "feels" accurate to you. The only purpose for revealing past lives should be to discover how they are influencing your present life, what the karma is that you need to work with, and how this information enhances your spiritual path this life.

Knowing who you were, what you looked like, etc., but not knowing the spiritual purpose behind that life is only of entertainment value.

A TIP ABOUT READINGS

All readings termed "psychic" are from the lower levels of the Universal Subconscious Mind. This means the reader is "reading" or sensing what you have stored in your subconscious, or interpreting what he or she feels you have in your subconscious. Clairvoyance, the ability to see the past or future events, is based on the fact that most individuals do not take active control of their own lives. Therefore most "psychic readings" can easily predict the future, since the individual will probably not change it. An aware person, however, is much more difficult to give a psychic reading, for he or she is very much *consciously* changing and growing.

Any psychic readings you have done should be thoroughly analyzed. Psychic fairs are not quiet events and the readers tend to be segregated into small booths that are not private. It is difficult for even the best reader to concentrate totally under these conditions, and this problem has to affect your reading. In addition, many (but not all) of these people depend on readings as a substantial part of their income, and they must give a percentage of their reading fees to the sponsor, plus pay for their booths. These people tend to push themselves to do as many readings as possible to cover all the financial outlay for being there. Again, this kind of pressure "to perform" can affect the outcome of your reading.

The other side of this issue is that some very fine readers can be available to you. You will need to seek those out as you become more aware and experienced in the metaphysical field, and have more trust in your intuitive self.

There are many different types of readings available, however we chose to give you the most common ones so that you can understand how these work. Readings are fun, informative, and can be very helpful at the proper time in your life. We do not discourage readings, only advise that you go to a reading with knowledge and your intuitive mind operating at full capacity. With this wisdom and awareness you will not be harmed psychologically, and can enjoy and use your reading. Your goals are to enjoy your reading and use it as a tool to guide you on your Spiritual Path.

METAPHYSICAL TEACHERS

Metaphysical teachers, like readings, come in all varieties. In fact we are all teachers and students. When you become somewhat knowledgeable about metaphysical information, you become a teacher whether or not you are teaching the public. A true metaphysical/spiritual teacher is always working on self first and foremost.

There are many levels of metaphysical teachers, just as there are grades in school. Some are very knowledgeable and have studied every metaphysical subject available, but cannot convey this knowledge to their students. Others have the same background and are eloquent in their delivery. Still others are self-righteous and demand that you study only with them or you are doomed to ignorance. They usually like to portray a mysterious air about themselves and pretend to have renounced the world. A little investigation into their personal lifestyle will probably reveal that this is not true!

There are other metaphysical teachers who appear very "earthy" in their presentation of knowledge and, again, like the mystical ones, you can tell if they are balanced in this "earthiness" by looking at their personal lifestyle. A truly spiritual person does not have to give up meat, responsible sexual intimacy, or money to be a good teacher, but he or she should not be abusing any of these things.

The best metaphysical teachers are able to admit their faults, continue to work on these, live a balanced life, and ALWAYS ENCOURAGE THEIR STUDENTS TO THINK FOR THEMSELVES. An honest teacher will not want followers, but will teach students to research information other than what he or she is teaching.

THE NEW AGE LABEL

Now let's talk about what the so called New Age really is. There have been many New Ages down through history and each one promised to bring enlightenment, whether it was the discovery of electricity, industrial tools, or the computer information age. So, you see, basically there is never really a "New Age."

For the metaphysical world the term "New Age" has an entirely different meaning. It means: *to live in an expanded consciousness acknowledging the oneness with our planet, humanity and all things.* It is that simple to define, and difficult to live. It negates prejudice of race, creed, or sex, poverty consciousness, and ignorance. Above all it supports continuous learning. Life long learning, changing and growing is all that is acceptable.

PAST LIFE THERAPY

Within the past several years, the concept of past lives has crept into the psychological community, and a treatment referred to as "past-life regression" is sometimes used to help people break through psychological blocks. The therapy works by regressing the individual, using hypnosis, to bring up suppressed "images" in his subconscious mind. He will be directed by the therapist to go to the images that are centered around the problem--called the "core issue"--that he is experiencing in the present life. Most often the mental images are set in different time periods, with the individual seeing himself in a different body, clothing etc.

Past-life therapists do not acknowledge the images as one hundred percent past-life remembrances, since they are not working with a metaphysical belief system. However, they do agree that it does not matter if you call the subconscious images past-lives or simply mental pictures. What seems to help the individual is reliving these images through regression, thereby coming to an understanding with the emotional incident that created his psychological block.

Not all psychologists use past-life therapy, as this is a recent type of treatment introduced to psychology by those who found regression very helpful. Those counselors who use past-life therapy have found effective healing of both the physical body and the psyche often takes place when traditional therapy has failed. Jungian psychologists particularly find this form of treatment fits quite nicely into their concept of archetypal images in the subconscious mind of the race.

An example of how past-life therapy can heal was demonstrated to the authors when we did an experiment with regression to help Deborah find the source of depression that she experienced every spring. Cognitive behavior therapy had helped her release her major depressions that plagued her for years, but every spring she still suffered a setback.

To our amazement Deborah found herself in a female body in the 1200's as a Cathar in France. The Cathars were a Gnostic sect considered heretics by the Catholic Church. The Cathars, as did most of the Gnostic sects, refused to convert to Catholicism and continued to practice their faith against the will of the Church. Much bloodshed and torture was used in an attempt to force conversion. In the end the military power of the Church won by attacking the last stronghold of the Cathars and marching 200 people down a hill to be burned at the stake.

Deborah's depression was a remnant of remembrance of this life and of being burned at the stake for a belief system she cherished in that lifetime. The depression always came in the spring because this was the time of year when the burning took place. Once she was consciously aware of this past life, and its influence on her mood, she was free of any major recurring depression. The past life regression therapy, in conjunction with cognitive behavioral therapy, gave her the insight and the skills to conquer her debilitating depressions.

A NOTE TO METAPHYSICAL STUDENTS

Change is a very frightening thing to most people because it means treading on unknown ground, which may also be uncomfortable until they have adapted to the terrain. For the most part people are unwilling to endure being uncomfortable for a short period, even if it means long term benefits. This is old thinking that threatens spiritual evolution by slowing personal growth.

Not everyone is willing, or ready, to accept the process of expanded consciousness and personal, spiritual growth. As a seeker of knowledge or student of metaphysics, this should not be your concern. By learning, growing and changing in subtle ways, you will be teaching much more than if you insist on dragging others along when they are not ready. Each person must follow his or her own path.

Metaphysics teaches that the personality is the only part of you that is your own, and that the subconscious mind is shared by all people all over the world. That means that input of billions of thoughts and images is recorded in the Universal Subconscious Mind every moment.

When the concept of past lives is added to the your own consciousness, you have eons of life experiences, thoughts, and images of those experiences available to you at the subconscious level. Not only are those images and thoughts at your disposal, but they are also available to anyone who can tap into the part of the Universal Subconscious Mind that reflects and reads your thoughts, past lives, and future events.

The "reader" or "psychic" is reading your mind at its very basic subconscious level. However, the subconscious does not always interpret the events from an adult point of view, but more from a child's perception. It is very influenced by doubt, fear, and desire. Therefore, someone reading your subconscious mind is may only be able to tap images of your fears, or desires for as discussed earlier, these fears and desires are thought forms created by your thinking. The person is reading and interpreting your thought images which may or may not be accurate.

You have free will and can change those thought forms to new thoughts that will be totally different than what the psychic told you would come to pass. A "reading" is the use of the psychic mind to fee or sense past, present, or future events.

The small percentage of "psychic readings" that predict events which actually happen is due to the fact that people can and should use their free will to create their own futures. Those who do not use their free will, but blindly accept what others tell them, will be the people whom a reader can "read" accurately. The reason for this is that the reader is interpreting only the fears and desires of the individual.

Problems arise if the individual believes what the reader sees is absolute true and it cannot be changed. He then "acts out" according to what the reader said would happen, because he believes so strongly that the reader is right. This is an example of the power of suggestion.

There are people who have trained to go beyond the lower psychic mind and can read, or interpret, the thoughts and past lives of another more from the spiritual point of view. The difference is important. Someone reading the higher mind spiritual energies has the advantage of getting beyond the emotions (emotional body) and thoughts (mental body) of the person they are reading. Emotions create powerful thought forms placed there by the thoughts and perceptions, but beyond those thought forms is the cause, or reason, they were created. Emotions are like an actor who plays his part, and then when the play is over, unmasks to become the person he is in real life.

The thought forms of strong emotions are masquerading as one thing, such as love, hate, or intolerance, when in reality they are often a mask for lust, anger, fear, or prejudice. That is why it is so easy for someone to say he or she is reading your mind. The "reader" is relating to the lower psychic mind and is actually feeling, and interpreting, your strong emotional thoughts of something, rather than the essence or truth about the matter which is much more objective.

The purpose of a reader is to give you truths you may not be aware of, because you may not be objective enough about your situation. By bringing these truths to your conscious awareness, the reader gives you information that you can use in conjunction with your own common sense to make a decision that is best for you.

It is always preferable that you learn to interpret for yourself what is best for your situation. When someone else tells you what they think the choice should be, or even what the choices actually are, you have given up some of your personal responsibility. As you grow spiritually you will connect with your own Higher Self, and its messages will come through to your conscious mind. Thus, by your own intuition, or through meditation and contemplation, you will become your own "reader" and not allow yourself to be dependent on another.

The psychic mind is a first step to becoming attuned to your mental abilities. It is a tool that you have and can learn to operate to give you access to higher mind energies, which eventually leads to conscious communication with your Higher Self.

It is not a phenomenal tool. It is a basic tool that all humans possess. It should be operated carefully and efficiently. Progressive training is required to learn to operate the psychic mind tool, and its use should not be looked upon with awe. The self-discipline required to tap into the psychic mind will reap great rewards in other areas of your life. You will notice greater productivity due to better concentration and peace of mind.

CONCLUSION

There are many metaphysical teachers, many metaphysical tools, and readings from which to gain knowledge. Have fun and explore these avenues, but remember to temper enthusiasm with a healthy dose of skepticism. Truth comes in many forms and each soul has the ability to find it when it is ready.

CHAPTER 9

APPLYING METAPHYSICS
IN DAILY LIFE

METAPHYSICAL STUDY AFFECTS YOU
ON A PHYSICAL LEVEL

The main purpose of metaphysical study is to put you in touch with your divine nature, called the Higher Self. This idea is not as esoteric as it sounds, for the mental tools used in metaphysics also work on a very physical level. You will go through changes as you study, for you will be confronted with and remove any mental blocks of prejudices, anger, fears, and resentments. Visualization, concentration, and meditation are the instruments used to remove these blocks. However, what you may not realize is how metaphysical study affects you on a physical level. As you work on your attitudes and meditate to achieve higher levels of consciousness, your body goes through a

112

change at the very deepest cellular level. Thus, metaphysical study affects you on a physical level, as does any spiritual study, or psychotherapeutic counseling.

As you remove mental blocks of fear, doubt, and low self-esteem, finer energies and higher forces begin to flow through you. You have an invisible electromagnetic field which lies over you called the "etheric double," and it is the same shape as your physical body. If you concentrate you can see it as a smoky blue layer over your skin.

CENTERS OF ENERGY WITHIN YOU

Within this etheric double are energy centers, or "chakras" meaning wheels. These invisible centers allow a flow of energy into your physical body. The centers are similar to little wheels that rotate at a speed normal for your body type and spiritual evolution. Each of us has our own set of centers operating at an individual rotational pattern.

The centers are a necessary part of you because they allow the invisible Life Force flowing down from the Deity to enter your physical body and sustain its life. Metaphysical texts teach that while your blood, body fluids, organs, etc. keep you functioning, it is this Life Force flowing through the centers that sustains the function of all body parts.

Based on this concept, whenever you practice metaphysical study, meditation, visualization, chanting, and prayer, the centers open gradually and your physical cellular structure begins to change, to adapt to the new life-giving forces coming into your body and mind.

Over a period of time with ongoing metaphysical techniques, you will go through a series of noticeable changes:

1. Any negative habits you have will become unpleasant to you, and you will feel a great urge to change them.

2. You will find you are more tolerant of others.

3. You will not get as depressed as you once did, however this is not to say you will not have your own negative emotions to work through. It will seem easier to understand and correct these.

4. You will be able to quickly "read" the motives of others.

5. Physically you will feel better. If there are any health problems present, you will intuitively know which physician, health practitioner, or methodology to follow to help you cope and/or recover. This does not mean you will be instantly cured; just that you will heal as much as possible, or accept what it is you are undergoing.

6. As your attitudes change and you become more positive and hopeful toward life, what you need and/or desire will come more quickly to you.

7. You will feel a deep and abiding faith in whatever you perceive the Deity to be; thus you will feel at peace within.

PROCESS OF HIGHER ENERGIES FLOWING THROUGH THE CENTERS

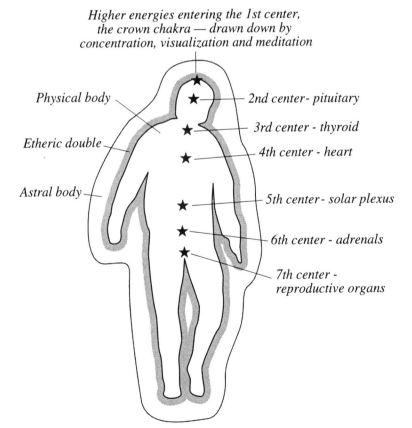

Higher energies entering the 1st center, the crown chakra — drawn down by concentration, visualization and meditation

Physical body

Etheric double

Astral body

2nd center - pituitary

3rd center - thyroid

4th center - heart

5th center - solar plexus

6th center - adrenals

7th center - reproductive organs

HOW TO APPLY METAPHYSICAL IDEAS IN EVERYDAY LIFE

1. Develop Concentration:

Learning to concentrate so that the mind is like a "laser beam" locked onto its subject will increase productivity. The ability to concentrate calms a worried or cluttered mind, forcing it to focus on one thing and putting all other things into perspective. With deep concentration you can begin to visualize effectively.

2. Be In The Now:

Focus your attention on the present moment, and do not allow your mind to wander. If you can do that, you cannot worry about yesterday or tomorrow because your attention is in the now. Ask yourself what learning experience the now is offering you; how can you help someone now; how do you feel about life right now? Can you keep your attention on what someone is saying to you without mentally drifting into past or future thoughts, or thinking of what you are going to say next? That is concentration, and if you are truly concentrating you cannot be distracted. When you are concentrating you are listening and focusing, which are the basic elements of meditation, visualization, and concentration.

3. Using Visualization:

Visualization is the greatest tool available for building a blueprint of how we want our lives to be. The art of visualizing is used in sports, healing and self-improvement programs. Concentration develops the ability to see clearly in the mind how we want to act, feel, or look.

4. Observing The Mind:

This exercise requires a few moments a day and will put you in touch with your psychological self. Sit as if you were ready to meditate and relax. Now with your eyes closed watch the patterns of your thoughts as they wander from one thing to another. Do you worry a lot about the past, present, or future? Is money, an intimate relationship, children, or a job the main focus of your thoughts? You can learn more about yourself than you ever believed possible by observing your mind. You can work on whatever issue, or issues, seem to be uppermost in your thoughts and learn to focus your thoughts away from these worries. If you have many fear thoughts and doubts, read principle number 5.

5. Wipe Out Doubt:

Doubt + worry = fear. The emotion of fear produced by doubt and worry is useless and destructive. Obviously a healthy amount of fear is required in physical life to protect the body from physical harm. However, to your Higher Self fear is a major block and a product of an undisciplined mind. To conquer fear, get rid of worry and doubt. In the Hindu sacred text of the Bagavad Gita, the main character, Krishna, representing the Higher Self, says: "Or if perchance thou believeth not these things and liveth in the illusion of belief in birth and death as realities- -even so, asketh thee, why shouldst thou lament and grieve? For, if this last be true, then as certain as it is that all men have been born, so it is certain that all men must die; therefore why grieve and fret thyself over the inevitable and unavoidable?" If you think about this question, it is quite practical.

If you could see the thought forms you create through worry and doubt, it would scare you to death. You may not be able to see them, but you certainly feel them in the form of fear and doubt.

Deny worry and doubt since you created these negative emotions. Use the word "cancel" every time you have a negative thought. Make up an affirmation to use after you "cancel" something. A good affirmation is: "I am a Divine Being, only good comes to me." Always see the lesson or learning experience within the situation or through an interaction with another person. Separate your facts about something or someone from the inner truth of the situation. It may be a fact that somebody is criticizing you, but the inner truth is that the person doing this is insecure and suffering from low self-esteem.

6. Listen To Your Intuition:

Most of the time you work out of your conscious, logical mind and call the intuitive feedback you receive from your Higher Self "just a feeling." When you learn to tap into those feelings and act on your intuition instead of just stuffing it away into a compartment of the subconscious, you are beginning to learn to flow with life and not fight it.

7. Eliminate False Guilt:

Western society seems to have a built-in guilt complex for every facet of life. Mothers feel guilty if they go to work before their children are in school. If you do something that is fulfilling to you, but your spouse does not approve you feel guilty. Children feel guilty if their parents get a divorce, as if it was their fault! There is guilt if you are a church-going individual and you do not go to church one Sunday. You feel guilty if you take some time for yourself without the family. There is guilt if after working hard to earn the money to get something you have wanted for a long time, you actually buy it. Certainly women have a most difficult time with false guilt, since they have been programmed to believe they should not be successful. However, men also suffer because their programming from society is that they have to be successful to be acceptable. Success is relative to your interpretation, and defined by your needs and desires.

What is successful for one individual may not seem so to another.

What has happened in our society that we have all this false guilt? The primary reason seems to be the "work ethic" we each grew up with. This is a series of erroneous messages that say: "You cannot be abundant until you have worked many long, hard years and retire;" "Money is the root of all evil;" "Mothers should not go to work until their children start first grade;" "Motherhood and being a wife is the most fulfilling thing a woman can do;" "A woman who wants a career really wants to be a man;" "To be a good parent you should spend every free moment with your children;" "To be a good wife/husband you should spend every free moment with your spouse;" "a man is not successful unless he is making $100,000 a year," and finally "It is selfish to do anything different than the above messages."

Whether you blame religion for giving you these messages, the government, your parents, or society as a whole, the fact is that they are manipulative, self-condemning and wrong. Western society and perhaps the societies all over the world, have never accepted the idea of growth and change. Anything that threatens the old ways of doing things and living are condemned by society. The reasoning behind the mindset of change being a threat is that if you change and the changes make you a better person, then that means those who do not change are wrong. The majority of the masses do not like to appear wrong or different, so it is easier to criticize and condemn those who are somehow different than it is to change. The status quo is more comfortable, even if it is not working, than changing to something unknown.

CONCLUSION

If you cannot apply what you have learned from any study, metaphysics or anything else, it is of little use to you. It merely fills your intellect with useless knowledge. Study = knowledge and application of study = wisdom.

Many people study metaphysical principles, but the ones who apply these are very few. The people who live by metaphysical principles are fewer still. Living what you believe, whether it is metaphysical thought or something else, is the key to a fulfilling life. Use metaphysical knowledge to make your life happy, flowing, and growth oriented.

CHAPTER 10

GLOSSARY

It is our goal to give you a text that translates meta-physical "jargon" into English, so that you may enjoy learning about metaphysical principles and not be intimidated by the terminology.

As you explore the bookshelves looking for one metaphysical topic that appeals to you, you will find many terms used to describe that one idea. A good example is the term reincarnation, which will also be labeled "past lives," "many lives," "life between lives," "Universal Laws of Reincarnation and Karma," and sometimes "transmigration." You can see how the terminology can confuse someone new to metaphysics or anyone investigating reincarnation.

This is by no means meant to be a complete guide of metaphysical terms. Metaphysics comes from many different systems of philosophy and it would take several books to cover all the terminology. Yet we did feel that a basic guide is essential for anyone new to metaphysical thought. Some words, such as chakra, are foreign and their origins will be explained.

With this in mind then, we present the following glossary which should assist you in reading metaphysical texts:

AFFIRMATION: A positive phrase or word said or thought repeatedly for the purpose of reprogramming the subconscious mind with positive thoughts. Using this method assists only positive thoughts to manifest into the physical plane. For example, an affirmation of health is: "I am healthy in all ways, body, mind, and soul."

ASTRAL BODY: The astral body is an invisible body surrounding your physical and etheric bodies, and usually stands out a few inches or a few feet from the physical body. The astral body is made up of fine energy but is dense enough to be seen by clairvoyants, or physically seen on black paper when a hand is spread out over the paper, and the lights are low, or off.

ASTRAL PROJECTION: Astral projection means to go out of the physical body and stand in the astral body. In the astral body you can walk about or project to any part of the world or universe.

AURA: An invisible field of light in different colors surrounding the physical body, and produced by emotions and thoughts.

CHAKRA: A Sanskrit word meaning a "wheel of energy" or center of energy. There are 7 chakras that lie over the physical body, within the etheric body. Their purpose is to bring in the invisible life force that keeps us alive and help us in our spiritual evolution. They are very connected with our endocrine glands and nervous system.

CHANNELING: Any form of mediumship is "channeling," which is actually interdimensional communication between this world and the inner dimensions, or those on other planets. Channeling is a form of telepathy between two intelligences, done by thinking images, words or symbols between the two minds. (See trance and mediumship.)

CLAIRAUDIENCE: Hearing telepathically. For example, you hear someone call your name but no one is around. Someone far away from you may have said your name, and you "heard" it across the miles. Another example is hearing your Spirit Guide "speak" to you, or hearing music from the astral planes as Mozart did.

CLAIRVOYANCE: The ability to see the future and past, as well as the ability to see auras and Spirit Guides.

CONCENTRATION: Used in metaphysics to mean focusing your mind so well on one subject that the mind produces a powerful mental energy like a laser beam to that subject. The purpose of concentration is to direct mental or physical energy to find solutions to problems, to visualize effectively, and to heal.

DIVINE SELF: A term used to describe the Higher Self, that spark within each of us that is divine and directly connected to the Deity. In psychology the Divine Self, or Higher Self, is represented by the superconscious mind.

ESOTERIC: A term meaning the deep, inner meaning of anything. Exoteric is its opposite term, meaning the outer, obvious, external or superficial meaning of something. Esoteric science is a term often used to describe aspects of metaphysics such as clairvoyance, telepathy, use of the Tarot, astrology, numerology, and techniques such as meditation, concentration exercises, and visualization.

ESP: Extra Sensory Perception, which we all possess. Sometimes called "the psychic sense" or "sixth sense." Basically, ESP is the ability to use the psychic senses of telepathy, psychometry, mediumship, and clairvoyance.

HIGHER SELF: Also referred to as the Ego, the Christ-Consciousness, God-Self, Divine Self and The Source. The Higher Self is that part of you that is considered your link to God, the Divine Spark within you which directs your actions, through your soul, to your mind and physical brain. It is like a director sending messages to help you grow spiritually. But until you become consciously aware of its presence within you, you may sense it as an "intuition" directing your actions. Learning to become consciously aware of its messages and to be in contact with it is a basic goal of metaphysical study.

HOLISTIC: Combining many different systems of study and techniques to accomplish something. For example, "holistic health" can combine medical science with massage therapy, herbs, homeopathy and meditation to heal.

HYPNOSIS: A state of mind where in the conscious mind is asleep, or bypassed, while the subconscious mind is awake and receiving information. There are many levels to the hypnotic state which can be achieved through the techniques of a professional hypnotist or self-hypnosis.

INNER DIMENSIONS: In metaphysics this is generally accepted as the many levels of mind; but it also means the levels of being beyond time and space. For example, Earth is said to be a three dimensional plane, and beyond that are other dimensions of existence. The idea is that other dimensions of consciousness exist, which have beings who are more or less evolved than humanity. "Interdimensional communication" is communication with those other beings, including those from other planets.

KARMA: Karma means cause and effect. Karma is neither good nor bad, but is the effect created by your thoughts, words and actions. The old saying of "what goes around comes around" sums up karma. Karma is created continuously by every thought, word and action, and is cumulative from other lives. For example, if you felt in a former life that boy children were difficult to raise and many times in that life said, "I don't ever want to have boys again!," that vow could possibly be fulfilled in the next life when you have only girl children. Another example is a life when you killed another in a dispute of some kind, and in the next life you work in a capacity serving that person in some way. In that life you might dislike him or her intensely without understanding why you feel this way. Karma is balanced as the two of you work together. You will experience whatever situation is needed for your to treat that person with respect this life, and forgiveness is accomplished on a subconscious level.

LIGHT BODY: This is your astral body, which if you could see it with your physical eyes, looks like a sparkling body of tiny, brilliant white lights. Its shape is identical to your physical body.

LOWER SELF: Also referred to as the ego (little "e," different from the Ego, capital "E" used to describe the Higher Self.) This term refers to your personality, your conscious mind, and your physical body. It is the part of yourself that requires the most discipline. It reacts rather than responds, can be over-emotional, easily distracted, and is concerned with the logical, rather than intuitive, point of view. When it is trained to integrate with your Higher Self, it is a most useful vehicle. It is a necessary part of you and is not to be looked down upon, but revered as the temple of the soul. The integration process of Higher Self to lower self is accomplished through meditation, spiritual study and conscious awareness of the effect of your thoughts, words and actions on the physical body and your personal environment.

MANIFESTING: The same as the dictionary definition, to bring something into being. In metaphysics, manifesting means to create with thought through visualization and see it "manifest," or happen, in the physical plane. For example, to visualize a vacation to Hawaii, and then to win such a vacation through a contest is a manifestation into the physical plane!

MEDITATE: The best definition of this term is to go within and listen. The purpose of meditation is to contact your Higher Self and receive its message. Meditation is also a tool for stress control. To meditate requires the stilling of the conscious mind and going beyond the images, fears and desires of the subconscious mind and daily living. Meditation gives you access to higher levels of mind where all knowledge is stored, and from which peace of mind flows. In healing, meditation is used to lower blood pressure, to build energy in the body, to steady the mind for better productivity and to reduce stress.

MEDIUMSHIP: In today's world, mediumship is also called "channeling." It is the ability to translate messages, or information, from one plane to another. The individual is then a "medium" between the planes or dimensions of communication. (See channeling.)

METAPHYSICS: The study of the human mind to act and know beyond physical reality. The study of metaphysics include the esoteric side of many other subjects, such as psychology, quantum physics, philosophy, theology, science and world religions.

OCCULT: Simply means hidden, or more specifically "hidden knowledge." It is not a negative term, as it has been interpreted over the years. Knowledge that is occult, or hidden, is information written in code or symbols so that those who would not understand could not access the power found in the occult information and abuse the knowledge.

PAST LIFE REGRESSION: The hypnotic state in which an individual is able to recall past lives, or images of another time period, in which he or she views him or herself as an active participant. The regression also brings up emotions and events of that time period, that can be resolved in the present life, for the purpose of psychological and often physical healing.

REINCARNATION: The principle or Universal Law of Reincarnation means that the soul of a human assumes a new physical body through many lives. The physical body deteriorates at death, but the soul has recorded all of the life experiences. After a time of assimilation of these experiences, the soul is ready to assume a new body and learn more of life's lessons, such as unconditional love, patience, forgiveness, a giving nature and the brotherhood of mankind. The body of the next life can be of a different sex than the former life so that the soul learns the differences between male and female expression. The purpose of reincarnation is to give the soul an opportunity to evolve back to the Deity after many lives of experiencing and growing on Earth and in other dimensions between Earth lives.

RELIGION: Generally thought of as a form of worship of the Deity and divided into many different styles and belief systems. In reality anything can be seen as a "religion" if enough people believe in it and structure their lives around it, such as art, psychology, music or cooking for that matter. There are recognized World Religions that are each a structured system of beliefs about the creation of the universe and a Supreme Deity. While metaphysics explores the form of religion, its main purpose is to put you in touch with spirituality, which may or may not exist in religion. Spirituality is the "spirit" of things, or underlying cause and purpose of humanity and the Deity's interaction with humanity.

RUNES: A set of stones or wooden disks with glyphs cut into them representing deep spiritual and psychological advice for a given situation. They are typically associated with the Norse culture, but actually are the result of many different cultures. A tool used for divining the future or understanding past and future events as a whole.

SOURCE: Sometimes called the "Divine Source" or "Source of All" and primarily means the Deity, whatever you perceive that to be. It is meant to be a spiritual term indicating that all energy comes from one Great Point, but which is so vast the human mind cannot conceive of It.

SPIRITUALITY: Spirituality is different from religion in that it has no labels, dogma or doctrine. It means the deep, inner belief system you have developed from your life experiences. Spirituality encompasses your perception of a Deity, what you think your purpose is for being on Earth and how you feel you fit into the scheme of nature and the Universe. (See Religion.)

TELEKINESIS: Ability to move objects with mental energy.

TRANCE: Very similar to hypnosis in that there are many forms of trance. Full trance means the individual is out of body (see astral projection) and is allowing the interdimensional being to speak through his or her vocal chords. In this form the medium often takes on the physical expression of the being. Automatic writing is another form of trance, where the interdimensional being uses the hands of the medium to write or type. A new form of trance, that will become popular as this decade proceeds, is called "Awareness Trance." This form of trance allows the medium to receive telepathic messages from the interdimensional being while the medium is fully awake and able to walk about. The Awareness Trance state allows the medium to operate from all levels of mind at once and access his or her own knowledge as well. This state draws upon information from two worlds, Earth and the other dimension.

UNIVERSAL LAWS: Mental laws set into motion at the time of creation, coinciding with natural law and working out of the psychology, emotions and psychic levels of the human mind. (See Chapter 2.)

VISUALIZATION: The ability to create mental images, of what it is you desire in your life. For example, visualizing a new home or a new career. Visualization is based on the metaphysical premise that all thought creates images, or thought forms, on the astral planes. When enough mental energy is added to these thought forms, they are "pushed" out of the astral plane into the physical plane as concrete manifestations of the thought. Visualization requires disciplined concentration and practice to be effective. It also requires that you know what you want, and ACCEPT RESPONSIBILITY for what your visualization manifests! As in all parts of metaphysical study, you do not have the right to visualize anything that will harm another.

A COMBINED BIBLIOGRAPHY and
READING LIST

UNIVERSAL LAWS

Holmes, Ernest, Science of Mind, Dodd, Mead & CO.,
1938
Andersen, U.S., Three Magic Words, Wilshire Book Co.,
1954
Keyes, Ken, Handbook To Higher Consciousness, The
Living Love Center, 1975
Ramacharaka, Yogi, Fourteen Lessons In Yogi Philosophy,
Yogi Publication Society, 1931

VISUALIZATION, CONCENTRATION TECHNIQUES

Gawain,Shakti, Creative Visualization, Whatever
Publishing, Inc., 1986
Hay, Louise, You Can Heal Your Life, Hay House, 1984
Joy, Brugh, Joy's Way, A Map For The Transformational
Journey, An Introduction To The Potentials For Healing
With Body Energies, J.P. Tarcher, Inc., 1979

REINCARNATION
Hall, Manly P., Reincarnation, The Cycle of Necessity,
The Philosophical Research Society, Inc., 1939, 1967
Atkinson, W.W., Reincarnation and The Law of Karma,
Yogi Publication Society, 1936

Algeo, John, Reincarnation Explored, Quest, The
Theosophical Publishing House, 1987
Guirdham, Arthur, The Cathars and Reincarnation, The
Record of A Past Life in 13th Century France, Turnstone
Press Limited, 1970

REINCARNATION--PAST LIFE REGRESSION THERAPY
Wambach, Helen, Reliving Past Lives, Barnes & Noble
Books, 1978
Woolger, Roger J., Other Lives, Other Selves, Bantam
Books, 1988
Fiore, Edith, You Have Been Here Before, Ballantine
Books, 1978

MEDITATION
Dass, Ram, Journey of The Awakening, A Meditator's
Guidebook, Hanuman Foundation, Inc., 1978
Baker, M.E. Penny, Meditation, A Step Beyond With
Edgar Cayce, Pinnacle Books, 1975
Easwaran, Eknath, Meditation, An Eight-Point Program,
Nilgiri Press, 1978

THE PSYCHIC MIND
Vishita, Swami Bhakta, Genuine Mediumship or the
Invisible Powers, Yogi Publication Society, 1919
Ramacharaka, Yogi, The Science of Psychic Healing, Yogi
Publication Society, 1937

Panchadasi, Swami, Clairvoyance and Occult Powers, Yogi Publications Society, 1937

de Laurence, The Master Key, The de Laurence Co., 1941

Curtiss, Homer F., Personal Survival, Curtiss Philosophic Book Co., 1946

Weed, Joseph J., Complete Guide To Oracle and Prophecy Methods, Parker Publishing Co., Inc., 1971

Agee, Doris, Edgar Cayce on ESP, Warner Books, 1969

Butler, W.E., How to Develop Psychometry, The Aquarian Press, 1971

DREAMS

LaBerge, Stephen, Ph.D., Lucid Dreaming, The Power of Being Awake & Aware in Your Dreams, Ballantine Books, 1986

Sechrist, Elsie, Dreams, Your Magic Mirror, With Interpretations of Edgar Cayce, Warner Books, 1974

Thurston, Mark A., Ph.D., How To Interpret Your Dreams, Practical Techniques Based On The Edgar Cayce Readings, Edgar Cayce Foundation, 1978

Taylor, Jeremy, Dream Work, Techniques for Discovering the Creative Power in Dreams, Paulist Press, 1983

WORLD RELIGIONS

Hall, Manly P., The Guru, Philosophical Research Society, Inc., 1972

Hall, Manly P., Twelve World Teachers, Philosophical Research Society, Inc., 3rd Edition, 1973

Ramacharaka, Yogi, Mystic Christianity, Yogi Publication Society, 1935

Three Initiates, The Kybalion Hermetic Philosophy, Yogi Publication Society, 1912

Smith, Huston, The Religions of Man, Harper, Colophon Books, 1958

Peterson,Roland, Everyone Is Right, A New Look At Comparative Religion and Its Relation to Science, De Vorss & Company, 1986

Pagels, Elaine, The Gnostic Gospels, Random House, 1979

King, C.W., The Gnostics and Their Remains, Wizards Bookshelf, 1973

Walker, Benjamin, Gnosticism, Its History and Influence, Aquarian Press, 1983

Stone, Merlin, When God Was a Woman, Harvest/HBJ, 1976

Eisler, Rian, The Chalice and The Blade, Our History, Our Future, Harper & Row, 1988

Incognito, M., The Secret Doctrine of The Rosicrucians, Yogi Publication Society, 1949

Prabhavananda, Swami and Manchester, Frederick, The Upanishads, Breath of The Eternal, Vedanta Press, 1978

THE SPIRITUAL PATH

Akhilananda, Swami, Spiritual Practices, Branden Press

Yogananda, Paramahansa, Autobiography of a Yogi, Self-Realization Fellowship, 1979

Chopra, Deepak, Unconditional Life, Bantam Books, 1992

Easwaran, Eknath, Formulas For Transformation, Nilgiri Press, The Blue Mountain Meditation Center, 1977

Fox, Matthew, The Coming of The Cosmic Christ, Harper & Row Publishers, 1988

Taylor, Terry Lynn, Messengers of Light, The Angels Guide To Spiritual Growth, H.J. Kramer, Inc., 1986

Gawain, Shakti, Living In The Light, A Guide To Personal and Planetary Transformation, Whatever Publishing, Inc., 1986

Roman, Sanaya, Spiritual Growth, Being Your Higher Self, H.J. Kramer, Inc., 1989

Roman, Sanaya, Living With Joy, H.J. Kramer, Inc., 1986

Redfield, James, The Celestine Prophecy, An Adventure, Satori Publishing, 1993

The Impersonal Life, DeVorss & Co., Publishers, 1979

Moore, Thomas, Care of The Soul, A Guide For Cultivating Depth and Sacredness In Everyday Life, HarperCollins Publishers, 1992

Levi, The Aquarian Gospel of Jesus The Christ, DeVorss & Co., Publisher, 1972

Dass, Ram, with Levine, Stephen, Grist For The Mill, Unity Press, 1977

Quinn, Daniel, Ishmael, An Adventure of the Mind and Spirit, Bantam/Turner, 1992